Speak Still

Published by 404 Ink Limited
www.404Ink.com
hello@404ink.com

All rights reserved © Wing Lam Tong, 2025.

The right of Wing Lam Tong to be identified as the Author of this Work has been asserted in accordance with the Copyright, Designs and Patent Act 1988.

All rights reserved. No part of this publication may be: i) reproduced or transmitted in any form, electronic or mechanical, including photo-copying, recording or by means of any information storage or retrieval system without prior permission in writing from the publishers; or ii) used or reproduced in any way for the training, development or operation of artificial intelligence (AI) technologies, including generative AI technologies. The rights holders expressly reserve this publication from the text and data mining exception as per Article 4(3) of the Digital Single Market Directive (EU) 2019/790

Please note: Some references include URLs which may change or be unavailable after publication of this book. All references within endnotes were accessible and accurate as of March 2025 but may experience link rot from there on in.

Editing: Laura Jones-Rivera
Proofreading: Heather McDaid
Typesetting: Laura Jones-Rivera
Cover design: Luke Bird
Co-founders and publishers of 404 Ink:
Heather McDaid & Laura Jones-Rivera

Print ISBN: 978-1-916637-14-6
Ebook ISBN: 978-1-916637-15-3

EU GPSR Authorised Representative
LOGOS EUROPE, 9 rue Nicolas Poussin,
17000, LA ROCHELLE, France
E-mail: Contact@logoseurope.eu

Printed and bound in Great Britain by Clays Ltd, Elcograf S.p.A.

Speak Still

Articulating the Silence of Bilingualism

Wing Lam Tong

Inklings

Contents

Prologue
Writing from the Realm of Silence 1

Chapter 1
Loss for Words: On Silence, School, and Society 19

Chapter 2
Feels Translated: On Silence, Selfhood, and Belonging 53

Chapter 3
Unspoken Lingua Franca: On Silence as a Common Language 77

Epilogue
Departing for Home 99

References *105*
Acknowledgements *111*
About the Author *115*
About the Inklings series *117*

To the ones who are finding their way home –

May this quiet book keep you company

Prologue: Writing from the Realm of Silence

If it weren't for my parents' decision that I must acquire a language they could barely speak, this book would never have been written.

My bilingualism began, as such, when my parents put a distance between us.

THE SPEAKING I

Nothing exists ahistorically – not ourselves, not our speech, not our silences.

I speak with a voice deeply embedded in history. Born in the 1990s, the last decade of Hong Kong as a British colony, I was raised in the liminal space between two cultures. Like a flower growing in the crevices, my voice took shape between the Chinese and the English languages.

Much like Hong Kong's story, which also began in-between.

Hong Kong, or 香港 (hoeng1 gong2)* as its Cantonese-speaking inhabitants call it, literally means *Fragrant Harbour* in Chinese†. Each time the city is called by its name, it is reminiscent of the harbour that cuts across its heart.

My earliest attachment to my city is with the currents of this harbour. Like all the other Hongkongers who went to a local primary school during the late colonial era, I was taught to appreciate the harbour by repeating a Cantonese singsong that meant *deep is the water, wide is the harbour; it's ice-free all-year.*‡

It was through those lyrical words I first learnt of the city's bildungsroman that took place long before I was born.

It sounds almost trite now that I recite it: it's the story of how, around this fine harbour, Hong Kong had grown from a fishing village into a trading port and into a metropolis. We were told to take pride in this old story nonetheless, for we were to follow the footsteps of our home and grow up by this shelter from the stormy seas.

---

* All Romanisations in this book follow the Linguistic Society of Hong Kong Cantonese Romanization Scheme, also known as Jyutping. Cantonese is a tonal language; the numbers 1-6 following each word indicates the word's tone. To learn more, jyutping.org/en/ is a helpful resource.

† Cantonese is a variety of the Chinese language. It is the most commonly used language by the Hong Kong population.

‡ In Cantonese, it was '水深港闊, 終年不結冰 (seoi2 sam1 gong2 fut3, zung1 nin4 bat1 git3 bing1)'

As such, I found my first sense of belonging in the waves.

But as I learnt later, Hong Kong's harbour is also a scar, cutting deep and wide across its heart – for its colonial history also began in this body of water.

According to historian John M. Carroll, when the British acquired Hong Kong in 1841, they were primarily looking for a trading base and an imperial outpost, and the deep and wide sheltered harbour served this purpose well.[1] A century and a half of colonial rule then followed, and the harbour has since been given the name *Victoria*.[§]

Across the time-space of 香港 and Victoria, its modern and historical names in Chinese and in English, Hong Kong became the bilingual city as we know it today, and its people began to live their lives between languages.

Like many Hongkongers, my first language – first in terms of time and proximity – is Cantonese, which I learnt from my parents.

I heard the first melodies of the tonal tongue from my Hong Kong-born mother, when she lulled me to sleep. My late father, who was born in Shenzhen, China and migrated to Hong Kong in the 1970s, was a Cantonese-speaking man well-versed in classical Chinese literature. He named me 穎琳 (Wing6 Lam4) in Cantonese, for

---

§ The Victoria Harbour, or in Cantonese, 維多利亞港 (wai4 do1 lei6 aa3 gong2). As a metonymy, Hong Kong is sometimes also referred to as the City of Victoria, 維多利亞城 (wai4 do1 lei6 aa3 sing4), which was originally the administrative, business, and cultural capital of colonial Hong Kong.

the words' literal meanings in *sprout* and *jade*, and their symbolism in the promise of growth and poise.

Our names are our first words. 'Naming is a difficult and time-consuming process; it concerns essences, and it means power,' writes Jeannette Winterson in her coming-of-age tale *Oranges Are Not the Only Fruit*.[2] I was brought into existence through a Cantonese name, and the tonal language became part of my essence. I was formed in the language, and my sense of self grew in it. My mother tongue would call me home by my name; I would respond instinctively to its calling. Each recital of my name would weave me deeper into the narrative of *who I am*, both to me and to my culture.

Over the years, I learnt to match the undulating tones in my parents' speech with the corresponding logograms in my storybooks. I also inherited my father's passion for the art of words, first by imitating the elegant strokes of the traditional characters, and later by fusing the words into stories and poems in Hong Kong written Chinese.¶

Cantonese, for me, is the language of home; or in Cantonese, I first learnt to find my way home.

English, on the other hand, is my language of departure.

My mum, who speaks basic English, started teaching me the English alphabet around the same time I began

---

¶ Hong Kong written Chinese is a variety of standard written Chinese, often used in formal settings, with a lexicon and syntax influenced by Cantonese and English.

conversing in simple Cantonese. The English language began for me as a primitive form of translation: the phrase *A is for apple* made sense to me because I had already identified the red fruit in Cantonese as a 蘋果 (ping4 gwo2), the snack my mum usually gave me after our afternoons in the park. And I was able to comprehend how *B is for boy* because I already knew of a 男仔 (naam4 zai2) (the Cantonese word for *boy*), an abstract idea brought to life by this playmate of mine who always took over the playground slide.

I acquired most of my first English words by way of my mother tongue and the memories I made with it, but I did so not because I needed to communicate in English as a clueless toddler. The reason why my mum taught me the alphabet song was to give me access to a world closed off from my Cantonese-speaking parents. For English was the language spoken by the esteemed members of society – the judges, the bankers, the doctors. If three-year-old me could recite all twenty-six letters, then I might have a better chance at getting into a reputable kindergarten, and in turn an English-Medium-Instruction school, and then a competitive university. Then I might get to live the more comfortable life my parents could not afford to give me with the struggling 茶餐廳 (caa4 caan1 teng1)** business they owned.

** A Hong Kong-style diner or café that serves affordable meals, teas, and coffees.

It all started with a mother's wish: through a language the parents could barely speak, the daughter might eventually sail into the outside world, far away from home.

In their seminal essay 'Critically Queer', Judith Butler discusses at length how one's subjectivity is formed, or how the *I* comes to speak. According to Butler, we find our voices in and through an ambivalent language that simultaneously enables and enchains us: 'Where there is an "I" who utters or speaks and thereby produces an effect in discourse, there is first a discourse which precedes and enables that "I" and forms in language the constraining trajectory of its will.'[3]

We can see this ambivalent language as the histories that we're born into, and the cultural narratives that inform our identities. As Butler describes elsewhere, we are all *culturally enmired* as a result.[4] Delving deeper into this imagery of a mire, language – or the narrative and discourse it propels – never exists in the clear. Every word has its own history, and language inevitably has past lives. Words have existed before us, as curses or blessings, slurs or cris de coeur, manifestos or decrees. As we wake up to our sense of a self, we are already swimming amidst everything that has ever been said in the past, which altogether constitutes our cultures and histories. We are always already immersed in this sea of utterances; yet it is also from this vastness we find the swells, the momentum, and the agency to draw our speech, our thoughts, our subjectivities.

It is in the sea that we come to be.

But where the sea is formed in colonial history and the resulting two tongues, those who dwell in it must speak through its undertows and rip currents.

My heartbeat is synchronised to the flow of my mother tongue. Without its tonal embrace, I would never have spoken. As for my English, it is a close speech first formed in the womb of my mother tongue yet eventually outgrew it.

Some call my English a *foreign* language. They say that if it is not *native* to me, then it can ever only come *second*. I'm kept behind an invisible boundary: English has become too distanced for me to claim as my own. Eventually, it turns into a drifting, dreamy silhouette that I must chase from behind, but like Achilles and the tortoise in Zeno's paradox, it is always one pulse away from my reach.

Even as I'm laying my languaged self bare in English now, it still feels less uninhibited than when I let my Chinese words flow out of me. As I write, I'm faulting my diction and second-guessing my grammar. I worry if the nuances in the metaphors I conceptualised in Chinese would come out as clichés in English. I worry that I would appear lost in time, disoriented by the many tenses of the English language, that I'm present at the wrong timing, regrettably late in finding out what happened in the past, and ignorant of things stretching on incessantly into the future.

Above all, I'm self-conscious. I worry if my English might be embarrassingly nonstandard, or, worse still, offensive to those who believe they have a more rightful claim over the language than me.

Thus, when I moved from Hong Kong to the UK in 2022 for my master's degree, and from *Cantonese and English* to *English only*, I encountered an abrupt loss for words. I felt stranded, like a fish out of water, being blocked from the vault of meanings originally formed in my mother tongue,[5] the headwaters that sustain my in-between eloquence. As the philosopher and psychoanalyst Julia Kristeva describes it, because of displacement, I have been cut off from the bittersweet slumber of childhood and become a stranger to myself, falling into a realm of silence.[6]

This is why I must attempt to articulate this silence now, in no other language than English: if English is the language that quiets me, then it is also the very language that will give me the voice and lived experience to speak of its mires.

The poet Wisława Szymborska once wrote, 'when I pronounce the word Silence, I destroy it'.[7] Pronouncing silence is the impossibility I'm confronting here: why am I estranged from a language I have known since childhood?

What are the entanglements that have drowned me in guilt, an inferiority complex, and speechlessness, and what has kept me from floating freely through my words? How can I anchor this language, and bring it home finally?

When my mother first taught me the English alphabet, it was in the hope that I could, one day, enter a world she had never seen. And this is the world I'm now venturing into: the one in which silence speaks.

A STILL POINT

I'm writing this chapter on a summer day in London in 2024, in a flat I have been trying to make into a home over the past year.

As the city undergoes a heat wave, I have left the window open for some fresh air. My building is an old gin distillery conversion that sits by the local high street, however – meaning that as much as I'd like, I'm not contemplating silence *in silence*. The melody of the everyday life counterpoints the making of this book: it's the muffled chitchats of passersby mixed with the giggling of school children, and embellished by some 2000s pop music playing in a lorry that just drove by.

I'm not writing from a quiet place. Our world has always been a clamorous one anyway. French philosopher and historian Michel Foucault believes that every word that has ever been uttered in history leaves a trace and remains in our world, marking it all over with discourse.[8] Dwelling in this world, not a single day in our lives would ever start in utter silence. There is always already a pre-existing, continuing process of words, words, words. These words form into language, and language into narratives, as we speak of them and carry on with our lives.

Across beliefs, cultures, and times, life begins in language and narratives. It could be born out of the worldmaking myth of Gaia, or that of Pangu, or the Genesis. Then life develops in narratives, with nations being founded upon legends, societies ordered around moral stories, and cultures made over shared tales. Life also becomes worth living in words: we invent new expressions to confess our love, say ancient prayers to mourn our losses, and tell fascinating stories of other lives and other worlds.

We are made in language, and we live in language. Or, as philosopher Paul Ricoeur poetically describes it, each of us is 'a tapestry of stories heard and told'.[9]

Yet, if we are to regard ourselves as a tapestry of tales, then what we won't be able to overlook is that some threads of our collective narratives are often recited more loudly, repeated more often, leaving more traces in this world.

This prompts the next questions: in this tale full of sound and fury that is our present reality, whose story has been left unheard? In our existing cultural narrative, whose voice has been muted?

These are big questions. But if we're honest with ourselves and with each other, the answer could be very simple.

We don't know.

For if our world is built upon the eloquence of *all things that have ever been said*, then, at the boundaries of this outspoken world, we come face-to-face with an unknown silence that consists of *all things that have not yet been heard.* On the brink of knowledge, we are at a loss for words. Our existing language is failing us. We find ourselves suspended at the still point of this tumultuously turning world.

What do we make of this silence?

Our existing language has long deemed silence as a formidable, meaningless void, and we have often seen silence only as an undesirable nothingness.

Professor Cheryl Glenn of The Pennsylvania State University, whose scholarship focuses on rhetoric and writing, describes Western culture as a talkative one, where speech is synonymous with civilisation.[10] Interestingly, even among those who are critical of the Western epistemic tradition, silence is still often taken with much apprehension for the powerlessness it implies. Audre Lorde, a self-described 'Black, lesbian, mother, warrior, poet', famously cautioned us about the fear of contempt, censure, judgment and annihilation compounded in silence. 'Your silence will not protect you,' Lorde said.[11] Speaking against the double subjugation of colonised women by both imperialism and the patriarchy, literary critic Gayatri Spivak likewise sees the resulting historical indifference as a form of silence: 'The subaltern cannot speak'.[12]

These are all significant remarks about silence, but as I see it, their significance goes far beyond what has been said. It is, in fact, the very act of *talking aloud about silence* that is important to me. For if we remember Szymborska, silence is a curious thing: as soon as we speak of it, even if as savagery or powerlessness, we break it.

It is the self-reflexivity involved in the articulation of silence that is transformative. Recalling the metaphor of language and culture as a mire in which we are born, each time we speak of silence, we are consciously calling out our embeddedness; in so doing, we are struggling to break free from within the mire. Think Peter Weir's *The Truman Show*: once we recognise that we are living in a construction, we start living in it differently. To speak of silence is thus an exercise of agency in and of itself, enabling us to resist the status quo, and to seek different possibilities.

From here, we can start speaking about silence differently.

When we are suspended at the still point, is it possible to see ourselves as being uplifted by it? In a world inundated with words, language, and narratives, silence could feel like a breath of fresh air, an escape from our inevitable historical embeddedness. Like any self-reflexive moment that would occasionally dawn on us in our mundane everyday lives, any suspension from our languaging lives is often transient. But each still point, however ephemeral, is still a break from the mire, still an exercise of our willpower against the given, still a punctuation put into a predetermined narrative of who we are and how we should live. If we all push for a still point often enough, a transformative collective silence could assert itself, one which could potentially change the rhythm of our existing narrative and shift the pace in which our world currently speaks.

The realm of silence, as such, is also the realm of unspoken words, unlived lives, unexperienced freedom. It is the vast land of the yet-to-know and the yet-to-be.

Silence, just like its outspoken counterpart, is a paradox. It enchains, yet it also enables. It fails, yet it also fulfils.

It's complex. It's ambivalent. It's human.

Now, if we return to the mundane summer day when I started this rambling about silence amidst the noises of the quotidian, feeling the subtle afternoon breeze finally coming in through the window, we can perhaps turn to the more temperate side of silence through our most ordinary human experiences.

In this clamorous world, don't we sometimes prefer quietness?

The quiet of early autumn mornings, of long walks by the river, of soft ambient background music.

The quiet of nods and smiles exchanged with strangers, of comfortable silences shared with loved ones, of hugs that readily forgive everything, no questions asked.

The quiet of not having to talk our way out of alienation, or defend ourselves against misunderstanding, or justify our existences against non-belonging.

In its multifaceted quietness, silence has inspired many mesmerising things: poetry, art, ways of life. In his poem 'The Quiet World', Jeffrey McDaniel imagines a world where words become a scarcity, and people must learn to love in silence by being content with listening to each other breathe.[13] In Chantel Akerman's 1975 slow cinema classic, *Jeanne Dielman, 23 quai du Commerce, 1080 Bruxelles,* silence suspends the need for a narrative and enables the film to morph into a meticulous study of domestic banality, humanising the muted existence of a widowed housewife, mother, and sex worker. In *The Artist Is Present*, performance artist Marina Abramović sat down in the Museum of Modern Art in New York in 2010 for three months. Whilst there, she looked deeply into the eyes of passing strangers. In their silent eye contact, they expose themselves to the vulnerability within human connection and the present moment.

Silence is malleable. If language is what forms cultural discourses and constitutes us as individuals and collectives, then silence is what permeates such language, flows across it, and creates new space in it by quietly weathering away its rigidity.

Silence is also diverse, in that it opens up what otherwise is set in stone to endless possibilities. To be rounded up like a smooth pebble, or to be broken down into unique grains of sand; to be washed up the shore, or to be carried away by the waves. Silence is the process that blurs the boundary between the sea and the land.

To enter the realm of silence, in this sense, is to willingly submit oneself to potential changes that incessantly contest static homogeneity. In bilingualism, this realm of silence could be found between the dynamic peripheries of the languages. If we immerse ourselves in this linguistic in-betweenness, its ebb and flow will reveal to us the subdued paradoxes and possibilities inherent in the way we communicate with each other. If we pay enough attention, we will see how the in-between speakers are slowly eroding cultural monism in their everyday oscillation between silence and speech.

Such is the position I'm taking for this book. I'm not a linguist, nor a critic of any sort; I'm just a speaker of my two tongues. The still point from which I speak is thus a personal place; as with most things personal, my experiences are often ordinary, and my feelings mundane.

But there is something significant about the trivial that is worth chronicling. In her book *An Archive of Feelings*,

Ann Cvetkovich observes how our everyday lives are rich repositories of feelings and emotions, archiving 'the force field around trauma, the low-level "insidious" way that it continues to make itself felt even at a remove from the experience itself'.[14] My bilingualism is undeniably the product of colonial history, and so to live an everyday life between languages also means living through the minute and tedious aftershock of this trauma, and witnessing how the past continues to haunt the present in various small ways. I will speak of it nonetheless, for the act of recognising and articulating a limitation is in and of itself a form of resistance.

To stand unwaveringly with the trivial is also to stand against forgetfulness. I've often been told that I'm wasting too much time pondering over insignificance. It's regrettably true most of the time, especially when it comes to my indecisiveness over dinner choices, or my inability to recover from random embarrassing moments from years ago. Yet, with many other things in life, I still believe in paying attention to the granular. Be it that slight feeling of being a misfit, or that nagging sense of non-belonging, the granular is what keeps us angular – such that we can resist being forced into predetermined narratives of who we are.

To appropriate the title of Adrienne Rich's poem, here is a cartography of silence for this book, chapter by chapter.

In Chapter 1: Loss for Words, I will start by going outwards. Mapping the English language education I received growing up in Hong Kong, I will outline the silences in the bilingual education system and, by extension, society. This topography of subdued voices will then take an inward turn in Chapter 2: Feels Translated, where I will consider the questions of displacement, selfhood, and belonging through the contours of my emotional life as experienced in translation. I will finally try to find a compass in Chatper 3: Unspoken Lingua Franca, by reimagining silence as a common language that will bring us all together in a world marked by a growing sense of unhomeliness.

This atlas of still points is written to find directions, in the hope that through our shared silences, we will ultimately orient ourselves, cross borders, and find our ways home.

Let's dive into this silence together.

Chapter 1
Loss for Words: On Silence, School, and Society

TWO TONGUES

We forget in different ways.

Memories are made, and then some of them go straight into oblivion, some become fragmented over time, and some slowly fade into hazy pictures. For the things I learnt in school, they have become half-forgotten by turning into hollow shapes of knowledge. I do remember studying the various types of clouds, for instance; but I can't recall any of the specifics, and I'm no longer able to tell if it's going to rain just by looking at the sky. I also remember memorising poems and feeling so deeply affected by them at the time; but they have now turned into blackout poetry in my mind, leaving only scattered words and phrases behind.

What has stayed over the years against my forgetfulness, however, are my bodily memories.

I still dream, every so often, of my teenage self walking up the slope to my school on the hillside, under the subtropical morning sun. Always sleep-deprived and always stressed out, I walk as I sweat in my white school uniform and blue cardigan. I'm always a bit out of breath, perhaps because of the slope, or because of this sense of urgency that perpetuates my dreams. In those recurring dreams, it always feels as if I'm running late to school as something important is about to happen. I will try to trudge uphill, yet a heaviness in my own body will weigh me down and hold me back. Unfailingly, I will get snapped back into reality with a palpitation before the dream can come into any sort of closure.

Over the years, the context has expanded, and I will find myself trying to run up the slope either to school or work or the hospital; but wherever I need to go, it remains out of reach. Then, as soon as I wake up, another day will have rushed in. Again, I will start rolling the boulder that is the daily grind up the hill and, again, I will become too busy to cast any second thought on the Sisyphus I turn into in my sleep.

It was the mid-2000s when I dragged my feet up that hill for school day after day. The handover of Hong Kong had taken place a few years earlier in 1997, and my city was, on paper at least, no longer a colony. I have only vicarious memories about the actual day when sovereignty over Hong Kong was transferred, for the grown-ups wouldn't stop talking about it. They would recount, over and over again and in great detail, how that turning point in Hong Kong's history arrived with a rainstorm that drenched the city and obscured its future.

As a child, I was mostly oblivious that an era had ended that summer. It is only with time that I realise how I have been shaped unknowingly by the aftermath of that historical downpour at the turn of the century.

Throughout my secondary education, I went to a Catholic girls' school a thirty-minute walk from the caa caan teng my parents ran. The school was by no means in the top tier academically, but it was a decent enough one my mother could get me into. It was aided by government funding, and more importantly, it was what Hong Kong people would colloquially call a 英中 (jing1 zung1), *English Secondary*, meaning a secondary school adopting English as a medium of instruction. In post-colonial Hong Kong, while Cantonese is still the most spoken language among the people, English and Chinese remain the city's co-official languages; and English-medium schools continue to be well sought after among parents and students.

My school was founded in a hilly neighbourhood with an aging population. The area was modest, but generally also safe and calm. Most of my schoolmates were from Cantonese-speaking local families from the working or lower-middle class; many of them lived in the public housing estates in the vicinity. For girls whose families had better economic means, their parents mostly favoured the school either for religious reasons, or for the humility for which its students were well-known.

Such humility, however, had always been accompanied by a sense of precariousness, centred especially around language. I remember being told repeatedly by our teachers that we needed to work hard on our English, and that we should not take our English-medium education for granted. This was something that would only dawn on me in hindsight, long after I had graduated. In the decade following the handover, schools were confronted with a competitive process to retain the right – or privilege even – to teach their classes in English.

This is because, in 1998, the Hong Kong government rolled out the mother tongue education policy at junior secondary level. Previously, in late colonial Hong Kong, individual schools could decide their own medium of instruction, and most students chose to attend English-medium secondary schools. However, the quality and effectiveness of teaching and learning in English varied, and in the 1990s the government began to limit access to English-medium education and to formulate a shift towards mother tongue teaching.

I found in the archives a guidance that the education department issued in September 1997, addressed to all secondary schools on their medium of instruction.

'For educational reasons, the appropriate MOI (Medium of Instruction) for most students is their mother tongue. For the benefit of our students, most schools should adopt Chinese for teaching all academic subjects,' writes the guidance. It was hoped that the mother tongue education policy would lift 'language barriers in the study of most subjects', leading to 'better cognitive and academic development' among the students, and in turn allowing more time for students to 'concentrate on the learning of English'. [15]

Students were nonetheless still expected to become fluent speakers of English for a pragmatic reason. As the guidance continues to explain, 'English is the language of business worldwide. To maintain a good standard of English is crucial to our economic competitiveness.' An important exception was thus made to the mother tongue education policy: some schools would be allowed to continue teaching their academic subjects in English, provided that they met the requisite standard of 'good results' in 'student ability, teacher capability, and support strategies and programmes'.[16]

The goal, ultimately, was for students to become practical polyglots who were 'biliterate and trilingual': mastering both written Chinese and English, and speaking fluent Cantonese, English, and Mandarin.

But as we know, language doesn't exist in a vacuum. It's culturally enmired, and so any language policy can only be properly understood with reference to its historical embeddedness. For a century and a half, Hong Kong was colonised by the British, and because of that, also by the English language. The language that was spoken among the traditional elites in the universities, the law courts, and the business world was predominantly English. Cantonese, on the other hand, had been the language of the ordinary folk and the everyday life. It was the tongue that one would hear most often when walking down the streets, in conversations in the caa caan tengs, or in family tête-à-têtes at home.

Even the colonial government admitted this cultural chasm in Hong Kong's languaging scene. As early as 1961, the government had identified a 'problem of language' in Hong Kong in the population census: 'English, which is the official language of the place and the language of a great deal, if not most, of commercial correspondence is understood only by 9.7% of the population'.[17]

Over the next decades, as free compulsory education was introduced and Hong Kong's economy grew, the number of English speakers in the city gradually rose to over half of the population.[18] Yet that deep-seated divide between the city's two tongues continues to render millions of Hong Kong bilingual speakers at least partially speechless today. This is the problem of language: as we learn to speak our languages, they are always readily situated in a historical stratification of culture and class. As the narrative of *who we are* develops around this hierarchical social order, a language binarism emerges. One language is elevated as the professional, and the other deemed as the vernacular. One promises to open you up to the sophisticated grandeur of the cosmopolitan world, while the other threatens to enclose you within the sheer banalities of the everyday.

Between our Chinese and our English, Hong Kong's bilingualism has taken on profound class and cultural implications that go way beyond language learning. It is a loss of innocence: even as we are learning the language as children, we already know that speaking English is not as simple and fun as the Disney readers or the episodes of *Gogo's Adventures with English* promise to be. We all realise, at some point in our languaging lives, that to become bilingual means to become eloquent and tongue-tied all at once.

In a society structured around language differences, the English we speak is too convenient a marker of our socioeconomic status, indicating our proximity to power and knowledge. Precisely because of that, English is an opportunity we must desperately hold on to, for proficiency in the tongue will determine our upward mobility. As soon as we speak, we are implicated in a linguistic prejudice: we are the victims, yet we are also the perpetrators.

How do we even begin to articulate all the contradictions in a language that simultaneously elevates and subjugates us? With such a historical scar at the heart of the city, could a pedagogical switch to the mother tongue alone ever be enough to lick its wounds?

The mother tongue education policy of 1998 turned out to be controversial among Hong Kong parents and students. In an article contextualising English-medium education in Hong Kong, applied linguist Stephen Evans summarised the public sentiments at the time. 'Many parents and students felt that the creation of what was inevitably perceived to be an "elite" English stream and an apparently "inferior" Chinese stream was high-handed, discriminatory and socially divisive,' Evans wrote. 'Given that proficiency in English is a prerequisite for entering higher education and for pursuing a career in the professional world, students assigned to the English stream were perceived to have an unfair advantage in life, while those allocated to the Chinese stream were denied access to valuable linguistic capital and therefore the prospect of educational and occupational advancement.'[19]

The surrounding popular discourse developed in the following years further entangled the language policy in its mire. Mass media reacted to the policy by coining the colloquial phrases 上車 (soeng5 ce1) and 落車 (lok6 ce1), literally meaning *getting on* and *getting off the train*, as shorthand for the medium of instruction sorting process. In the news, schools that got to retain or switch to English as their medium of instruction would be congratulated for *getting onboard*, while those that failed to meet the relevant requirements and had to start teaching their subjects in Chinese would be described – sometimes stigmatised even – as having met with misfortune and getting ousted from the Elitism Express.

What followed the introduction of the policy was a frenzy. Local students who had to rely on government-funded public education now faced fierce competition: after evaluation, the government decided that only 114 schools, which amounted to only one-fifth of secondary schools in the city at the time, were qualified to teach its academic subjects in the English-medium.

That wasn't the end of the story. Some of the English-medium schools later decided to become semi-private by collecting a school fee besides receiving government subsidies to retain autonomy over their student recruitment, curriculum design, and medium of instruction, via the Direct Subsidy Scheme. In other words, these schools could teach their classes in English to selected students with minimum official interference. This created further boundaries within boundaries: the Elitism Express now has a first class compartment with exclusive seats.

To use the language of the media back then, I was among the fortunate ones. My school was one of the government-aided secondary schools that made it on board – although only marginally, as the train doors were closing. In the initial round of government decisions, my school didn't get to retain its English-medium status, and only reclaimed it on appeal after a year of hard work proving its English teaching and learning capabilities to the authorities. This might be where that lingering sense of precariousness came from: it was the aftershock of having been deemed inadequate, of having been turned away, of having to prove one's worth only to lay claim to a language.

Amidst all the commotion, the train departed. Secondary education in Hong Kong began to bifurcate in language.

MONOLINGUAL MONOLITH

'Growing up, we worked so hard to drill a grammar checker into ourselves,' Deborah tells me with a small smile as she lets out a sigh. 'But now, we work even harder to stop it from scrutinising everything we want to say.'[20]

I meet up with my friend Deborah after she has had a long day at work. Deborah is an English teacher at a government-aided primary school in one of the most rapidly gentrifying neighbourhoods in Hong Kong. The school sits right next to a large public housing estate that is surrounded by luxurious homes in skyscrapers. Most of the school's students are from Cantonese-speaking working class or lower-middle class families, and are learning English as a second language.

Deborah and I met each other long before she became Miss Deborah, the stern but gentle teacher to her students. We went to the same secondary school, and sat next to each other in our A-Level history classes. A camaraderie soon developed between us as we prepared for the stressful university entrance exam, and we bonded over our mutual ability to understand each other. Deborah was gifted at deciphering the battles and revolutions I doodled with crude stick figures all over her history notes; and I was exceptional at decoding the tender shrewdness masked under her stoic demeanour.

I tell Deborah that I'm writing a book in English about my English, or more precisely, *our* English, for we learnt it the same way. She then makes that remark about our inner language critic.

'At least a grammar checker is nice and helpful,' I say. It has taken me a moment to gather a reply, searching in my lexicon for the right words but to no avail. 'The thing that we internalised? It's just harsh.'

I have resigned to saying something vague again, trusting that Deborah can always decipher the abstract. For there is a tacit understanding between us, even when that *internalised harsh thing* has rendered me inarticulate.

We share a common language beyond all our Chinese and English words, acquired not only through the years we spent reading each other's abstract doodling and suppressed emotions, but also from our shared experience growing up in the same liminal space structured by the same history, constrained by the same discourse, and ordered by the same system.

This is exactly what makes it necessary for me to speak of the limitations over our speech now. To carry on with this book, I must illuminate the tacit for me to traverse those constraints that have failed my words.

It's not an easy task, however. To form my thoughts into sentences, I'm first confronting my anxiety about my grammar. The English grammar is, of course, the foundation and structure that has built the language, but where the parts of speech and tenses have been drilled into us through endless quizzes and exercises, in a binary of pass-or-fail and right-or-wrong, those cornerstones of language have turned into stumbling blocks.

I have learnt grammar not as the bedrock that supports my speech, but rather as draconian orders: any slip of the mother tongue would threaten to encroach my English. How do I begin to speak then until I feel I have complied with all its commandments? *Pluralise your English nouns!* Even if in Cantonese the signifier of the object stays static when it multiplies. *Gender your pronouns!* Even if the mother tongue doesn't discriminate and would have addressed everyone and everything as the same. *Relearn your sense of time!* Your past, present and future must now take place in the very action, at the conjugation of the verb; it should no longer wait, as your mother tongue would, for time to reveal itself in sentence-final particles at the end.

Even when I have got my grammar right, my accent would continue to keep me tongue-tied. To get rid of the Cantonese accent in my English, I have been trained to embody another way to speak: moving my mouth in different ways to imitate the intonation, rolling my tongue to mimic the sounds that do not exist in Cantonese.

But whose English am I embodying? And whose accent am I imitating?

'We were all just trying to sound *native*. Whatever the word meant.'

'It meant *white*,' Deborah shrugs. 'We didn't even know native speakers could be not white.'

As embarrassing as it is for me to admit this now, we honestly had no idea.

Hong Kong has, of course, always had a culturally and ethnically diverse population, but the city is too socially stratified for kids like us to register its multiculturalism. We grew up in a largely homogenous community, where our teachers and schoolmates were predominantly Cantonese-speaking Hong Kong Chinese. The only point of real-life reference we had as to what *nativeness* in the English language meant was the NETs in our school.

NET stands for *Native-Speaking English Teacher*. It has been the Hong Kong government's policy since 1998 to fund public-sector schools to hire NETs, who are tasked with enhancing students' exposure to English. The official definition of a NET is, to be fair, quite broad: a NET should be either a native speaker of English, or someone who possesses native speaker-level English competence.[21] In practice, back in our day, NETs were often hired overseas from what linguists called 'the inner circle English-speaking countries', such as the UK, USA, Australia or Canada; the candidates who eventually got chosen by schools were often white.

Deborah and I were taught by a few different NETs back then; they often came and went. One of them was A. A was a cheerful, laid-back Australian man in his late thirties who remembered each of his students' names. Unlike our other classes which often felt stressful due to a curriculum overload, A's English lessons were much more interactive and relaxed. Most of the time, all we were expected to do was to speak to him in English.

As part of its English teaching and learning initiatives, our school used to sign its students up for a city-wide interschool speech competition every year. One year, several of us were representing the school for a dramatic scene recital, and we were assigned an excerpt from the final chapter of Charles Dickens' *A Tale of Two Cities*. As the designated native English speaker at our school, A became our coach.

Our group started spending many afternoons after school in rehearsals. Sometimes we rehearsed in the computer room, sometimes in the school laboratory, sometimes at the back of the school hall. None of these made the fanciest venue for reading Dickens, but all other classrooms in our small school were occupied for either remedial classes or after-class tests, and like the Hongkongers that we were, we just had to make do with any space we could find.

We were a bunch of shy, taciturn teenage girls who, truth be told, didn't particularly enjoy public speaking, but we put in the effort anyway. We would read the excerpt, line by line; and A would listen, jumping in from time to time to correct our pronunciations and polish our intonations along the way.

The murmuring of many voices, the upturning of many faces, the pressing on of many footsteps in the outskirts of the crowd – so we repeated mindlessly after A.

Before that excerpt, the only Charles Dickens we had read at the time were the abridged versions of *A Christmas Carol* and *Oliver Twist* for our book reports. We didn't know much about the author, let alone the political turmoil and social inequalities that motivated his writing. We were largely unaware of the historical context of the novel we were reading aloud, and so we were also oblivious to the fact that those many voices and many faces were crowding around the guillotine to watch death.

As we indifferently repeated Dickens' counts of death for the umpteenth time, something else dawned on me instead.

We didn't sound like A, I suddenly realised.

I was sitting at the back listening to my classmate speak when this jarring epiphany hit. However hard we tried, we weren't speaking like A. Something was off, either in the intonation, or in the enunciation of the vowels, or in the missing final consonants. I could still hear the Cantonese in our English voices, and that made me self-conscious, as if I was listening to a recording of my own voice.

I was bewildered, realising for the first time that we had no control over how we spoke. That we couldn't sound the way we wanted ourselves to sound. That our Cantonese, our mother tongue, our language of home, had got in the way of our approximation to what we considered good English – the native speaker's English.

It took me years to figure out that it wasn't an accident that a non-native English speaker would feel this way.

The native speaker concept is culturally enmired in a presumed monolingualism. Linguistic purism is often problematically entangled with our definition of language proficiency, ironically putting a multilingual speaker at risk of sounding like a language failure. Linguist Li Wei points out a common misconception about language in our cultural discourse: that 'having languages other than English in one's repertoire, even if from birth, somehow dilutes one's competence and raises doubts over one's entitlement to the claim of a native English speaker'.[22] Cultural critic Rey Chow has made a similar observation. Having an accent in one's spoken English, as Chow puts it, is often considered 'an incomplete assimilation, a botched attempt at eliminating another tongue's competing copresence'.[23]

In fear of diluting our English competence, we begin to draw a careful distance from our mother tongue. We begin to compartmentalise our languages. We begin to impose on ourselves a contrived monolingualism.

As part of the mother tongue education policy, it was an express government directive to 'discourage the use of mixed code, i.e. a mixture of Chinese and English, in teaching and learning.'[24] So, out of the best of intentions, my school did all it could to simulate a monolingual environment for us. No Chinese should be spoken in the English classroom. Our head English teacher, despite being a Cantonese speaker herself, insisted on ever only speaking English to her students. Outside the classroom, there were English Days every week where the whole school was supposed to converse only in English. While watching too much television was generally discouraged, *practising our English listening* became the handiest excuse for us to make exceptions to the rule, and legitimately spend hours in front of the computer watching episode after episode of *Gossip Girl*, *Supernatural*, *Doctor Who*, and *Buffy the Vampire Slayer*.

Our experience of language compartmentalisation is far from unique: it is a recurring phenomenon across time and cultures under the shadows of imperialism. In history, it had sometimes gone much further than mere compartmentalisation, driving people into segregation or opposition even.

In his essay 'Between Worlds', Palestinian-American philosopher Edward Said recalled his encounter with an 'unjust colonial stricture' in the elite English school in Cairo he went to from the late 1940s to early 1950s: 'the school's first rule, emblazoned on the opening page of the handbook, read: "English is the language of the school; students caught speaking any other language will be punished."'[25]

Similarly, Kenyan author and academic Ngũgĩ wa Thiong'o also experienced language stratification. He described the harmony between the language of his education and that of his culture as being broken when English became the elite language which 'all the others had to bow before it in deference' in 1950s Kenya. In his colonial school, students caught speaking Gĩkũyũ would be subject to corporal punishment; and, in stark contrast, any achievements in English would be rewarded by prestige and applause.[26]

It was along this deep gulf between the English language and the mother tongue that Hong Kong also experienced a traumatic rupture. The bilingual city is thereafter split into two unequal halves: part English, part Chinese, with a rift in between to prevent the mixing of the two. It is the fault line that first cuts deeply across society, separating the ruling elites from the people. It then runs through the education system, pulling the schools apart in language. Over time, the fissure digs itself into the city's bilingual inhabitants, drawing an arbitrary boundary to separate the words that have brought them into existence.

For institutional learners of English as a second language, the language boundary is internalised as a red line that we should never cross. We learn that speaking good English means having to watch our tongues, segregate our thoughts, and keep our languaged selves apart. We learn that anyone who crosses language boundaries risks compromising their future abilities to surmount more profound divides in life. Those Chinese words and phrases in an English conversation could get you shamed for speaking Chinglish. Confusion between Chinese and English grammar could hold you back from higher education. The Cantonese accent in the way you speak English could trap you behind class barriers forever.

You have been warned: Don't Code Mix. Be bilingual, but never in unison. Speak, but stay split, as if you were two monolingual speakers living in one person.

Angel Lin, professor of English language education at the Education University of Hong Kong, describes this monolingual mode of English learning as a 'one-classroom-one-language pedagogical straitjacket'.[27] This is an unsettlingly apt image: we are bound by a homogenous, rigid, and inapproximable concept of what English proficiency means, with any attempt to break free too quickly stigmatised by our social discourse as broken English. Any uninhibited way of speaking the language, including code-mixing or embracing our natural accents, in turn becomes culturally pathologised as inferior, unsophisticated, and nonstandard.

There is also something uncanny in Lin's metaphor that only a Chinese-English bilingual speaker could notice. Pathologisation is, in fact, exactly how we refer to a solecism in Chinese: 語病 (jyu5 beng6), a *language ailment*.

For fear of catching language ailments, people just stop speaking.

Perhaps, as teenage girls, we weren't so shy and taciturn, but we would rather smile awkwardly in silence to each other than trying at small talk on English Days, just so we wouldn't get judged for our accent. We would rather joke that we didn't know how to speak 雞腸 (gai1 coeng2)†† and keep our mouths shut than to make a fool of ourselves with wrong grammar. We would rather stay ignorant of Charles Dickens and his social realism than to be ridiculed by the reality that, in our own context, those who could read and understand Dickens were usually the socially privileged ones.

'You'll have to leave your mother tongue, from here on out living in a language acquired in school via exams and inferiority complexes,' writes Hong Kong writer Wong Yi 黃怡 in her short story 'Overseas Bride', where she captures the poignant speechlessness in Hong Kong's bilingualism through the tender narrative voice of a lover.[28]

It's a language we acquired against all odds, but we didn't acquire it to be romantic. We didn't acquire it to tell our life stories or to write poems to each other. We also didn't acquire it to articulate the frustration we feel when a word gets stuck behind the cultural boundary on the tip of our tongues.

As Angel Lin puts it, the language we acquired has become a monolithic, pre-packaged commodity delivered as if in a transaction to prepare students for the high-stakes, standardised testing regimes.[29] The years we have spent learning English in simulated monolingual

---

†† Literally meaning 'chicken intestines', 雞腸 is a colloquial Cantonese metaphor for the Latin-script alphabets, and by analogy, the English language.

environments culminate in the university entrance exam, the one chance that we get to convince the highly selective system that we have finally become the practical polyglots our capitalist society needs.

Public exams in Hong Kong usually take place in what we call a 回南天 (wui4 naam4 tin1), *the dampness resurgence season*. It is when spring brings so much warmth and humidity back to the subtropical city that water drops start dripping down the mirrors, the doors, the walls, everywhere.

Year after year, in this suffocating stillness, our students take the test.

Despite all the ways there are for me to forget, I do remember my English writing exam. I was sitting in the hall along with hundreds of other students who had gone through the same system and learnt the same drill. In front of each of us was a piece of exam paper and an answer booklet, which were damp to the touch because of the humidity. We must not turn them over until it was exactly 8:30am. After the invigilators had made the standard announcements, the entire exam hall waited for the clock to tick in silence. I was a little dizzy from the lack of sleep the night before, but before I could even think about how I feel, the clock struck half past. Our docile bodies reacted instinctively. In one swift, uniform motion, the entire hall flipped the exam papers open and started writing ferociously.

There is a well-known Chinese saying which translates into English as 'Strict teachers produce outstanding students'. What is your opinion?[30]

It was a metafictional moment, almost corny now, but it was an actual essay question from the exam I took. An outstanding student trained by strict teachers would know exactly how to write for a good grade. It was all about writing with perfect grammar, lack of spelling errors, balanced arguments, avoidance of overused stock phrases, appropriate use of idioms. An outstanding student would know that their writing did not necessarily have to do with their honest opinions.

After our A-Levels, I stayed in Hong Kong to read literature and law, while Deborah initially left for Sydney for university, before coming home and eventually becoming an English teacher.

I ask if Deborah remembers what she wrote in that essay over a decade ago.

'Of course not.' Deborah shakes her head, propping her chin on her hand.

We have also already forgotten what we really wanted to write. The strict teachers and the outstanding students – by whose definition, and at what cost? Those considerations were too risky to be relevant at the time. Even as eighteen-year-olds, we already knew too well what we were tested for, and we certainly would not risk our grades with how we truly felt. If we, as the angsty teenagers that we were, could speak freely, what would have been said?

We thought we could wait to speak. Until the tests were over, until we got into university, until we found ourselves a decent job and got out of the education system.

But now we no longer remember what it was that we wanted to say.

We have grown up to find ourselves stranded at the rift between our bilingual mind and the monolingual monolith. Our speech has become dissociated from our thoughts, and our cultures estranged from our senses of self. We approach and project who we are by othering ourselves, or as Ngũgĩ wa Thiong'o puts it, we speak from 'the point of view of alienation, that is of seeing oneself from outside oneself as if one was another self'.[31]

We are made in language, yet part of that language is taken as an expediency. We don't mean what we say, and we don't say what we mean. Over time, the excesses of our meanings and intentions dissipate into silence and become irretrievable.

What remains with us, then, are the truncated thoughts and half-hearted utterances that we made do with, in hollow shapes of language.

IN-BETWEEN ELOQUENCE

Whilst studying at university, I had a side hustle as a private English tutor.

For a year or two, this was my routine: on a weekday afternoon, I would travel across the Hong Kong Island from my university at Pokfulam to a residential neighbourhood in Taikoo Shing to meet with T. T was a primary schoolboy obsessed with *Minecraft* and *Star Wars* who wanted to become a doctor when he grew up. On Sunday mornings, I would spend time with G at her home at a firefighters' quarters near Ngau Chi Wan in Kowloon. G, a teenage girl in senior secondary school, had set her mind on becoming an architect.

They both called me *Mit1 Si4*, the Cantonese transliteration of the English word *Miss*. It felt strange at first to be seen as a teacher, when I had ever only been a student all my life. I had doubts if I qualified at all: I had no real knowledge to give, except perhaps a few survival tips in the education system, but I posed as a *Mit Si* for the job anyway. T and G had made things easy for the teacher-imposter fortunately: they were the most patient and dedicated students anyone trying their hand at teaching could hope for.

My tutorial classes weren't fun, to say the least. For T, I was hired to deal with his English homework, of which there was always too much. T went to one of the most competitive semi-private primary schools in the city, and already had another English tutor – a native speaker – to train his spoken English. My main job was to trudge through the endless spelling worksheets and reading comprehension exercises and grammar workbooks with him. As for G, I prepared her for her university entrance exam. G was working incredibly hard to get into an architecture programme, but worried that her English grades would get in the way. Every Sunday, I repeated with G the strict revision drill I went through: we worked on decades' worth of past papers, memorised lists of vocabularies and phrasal verbs, and wrote and rewrote dozens of practice essays.

I quit tutoring when I graduated from university, in the summer before T got into secondary school, and G began her architectural studies. After a long, tedious struggle for all of us, that summer marked a jubilant milestone in our lives. As with most turning points in life, however, too often we focus on the loud, celebratory moment, and neglect the long metamorphic silence preceding it. In hindsight, our transformation is always in progress, albeit quietly.

I now see how, by calling me their *Mit Si*, T and G did put me in a special position. Not one of hierarchical authority, for they knew full well I was just a student myself, no more than a few years ahead of them in the examination race. The symbolic significance of *Mit Si* lies, instead, in how that word is made. In an act of transliteration, *Mit Si* is coined with the double and the in-between: the word is at once Cantonese and English, and its meaning constituted between and beyond those two ways to speak.

That was precisely how we found our ways through words together.

Despite our generally monotonous routine, every now and then, T's teachers at his school would assign him a piece of free composition, and that would brighten up our afternoon. T might be trapped in front of his writing desk, but the boy was an exuberant, free spirit deep down, and was never short of ideas for adventure stories. I would give him a pencil and ask him to just write, and he would, all afternoon. The boy could write for pages non-stop. When his English failed to catch up with his imagination, he would Romanise a Chinese phrase and carry on. When the expanse of his thoughts grew too big for his existing lexicon, T would turn his exercise book into a graphic novel, soldiering on with his story with the *Minecraft*-inspired hieroglyphs he invented. It was only when the hero in his epic finally needed a rest that he would stop and ask me to read. Then we would work together to translate the saga back into a known language, under the textbook monolingualism required by his school teachers.

In those quiet, wearisome mornings when G was relentlessly writing on the mock exam papers, she would sometimes break the silence and ask, in a soft voice, *Mit Si, how do I translate this?* Sometimes she would present me with a word I have in my English vocabulary; but more often it was more challenging, like a 四字成語 (sei3 zi6 sing4 jyu5) *four-character idiom* in Chinese. When no equivalent words were readily available, we would take a break from the rigidity we were busy complying with, and put our heads together to make meaning. Following G's architectural instinct, in that neat and tidy handwriting of hers, we would carefully deconstruct the familiar phrase in our mother tongue, and find a way to convert, expand, or reconstruct it in the English language as parables, proverbs, or metaphors.

Those were significant languaging moments. In T's unbounded adventures in his language innovation, or in G's meticulous bridging of her two tongues, we were experimenting with language and had not spoken yet. In those moments, we were still living in our natural bilingual mind. Formal education had not yet fixed our words-to-be, and the monolingual monolith had not yet tamed our meanings-to-come.

We dwelled, even if fleetingly, in the ambiguous borderland of meanings, in the pregnant pause before speech, in the equivocal silence before utterance.

Those moments illuminate how bilingual speakers can see the rift between mind and language differently: the abyss reveals itself as an underexplored, free-flowing liminal space, the repository from which we draw our meanings from all our languages fluidly.

People have come up with many labels to describe our dynamic, in-between ways of meaning-making: transliteration, code-mixing, code-switching, pidgin, creole. In Cantonese, we call it 中英夾雜 (zung1 jing1 gaap3 zaap6), a term that vividly describes the in-between idiolect of many Hong Kong bilingual speakers as a *Chinese-English mishmash*.

The system does not like the mishmash. Through both its official pedagogy and the cultural discourse so created, formal education has long stigmatised the mishmash as chaos.

However, if we could ever find the patience to listen a bit more closely, suspending ourselves momentarily from the judgment of the tumultuous cultural discourse around our speech, we would begin to discover the many meaningful nuances in our gaap zaap language.

Our two tongues crisscross to create fuller meanings, as in T's languaging escapades. We translate for new connections, as in G's construction of language bridges. We also mix the codes to stir up new ambiguities. For Cantonese sentence-final particles have emotional implications, adding them to a simple English sentence can destabilise and multiply its meanings. The assurance suggested in *it's okay*, for instance, would subtly change into ambivalence when we say *okay* laa1, or even suspicious unease in *okay* gwaa3. In some other occasions, we cherry-pick our codes to change our register. My father used to insist that I apologise by saying 對唔住 (deoi3 m4 zyu6) instead of *sorry* for my mischief, for he felt that the former would come from a more sincere place in my heart. *Love* and 愛 (oi3) might refer to similar affections, but for us the words could carry different weight: a confession made in English could sometimes be easier to utter than its solemn-sounding Cantonese counterpart.

This mishmash of language modalities at once enchains and enables. It no doubt has its roots in our colonial past, but it is also the headwaters from which we in-between speakers draw our heterogenous eloquence. Like the rise and fall of the tides, the flow through which each of us comes to speak is constantly changing, depending on the context.

It is through this wave-like, fluid bilingualism we confront our linguistic inequalities. We find a liminal position to counteract the arbitrary and traumatic language segregation, and we acquire an inherently diverse voice that calls monolingual supremacy into question.

As we speak, our languages blend, blurring cultural boundaries and breaking the silence pressed upon us by colonial alienation and internalised estrangement.

Observing the way multilingual speakers organically think and communicate with each other, linguists have conceptualised a critical possibility to speak beyond boundaries by taking our differences as the norm. They call it *translanguaging*. It is an idea that sees language as an evolving process that is full of life: translanguaging understands all our meaning-making modes as one repertoire, from which we draw our thoughts and create our speech. In this versatile, abundant repertoire, our words become boundless, resisting the hierarchical construction of *first* or *second language* and contesting the essentialist labels of *mother tongue* or *native speaker*.

It is when we take the social and cultural burdens off our words that our words can float, and sweep cross the barriers.

Seeing this radical, border-crossing potential of our fluid multilingualism, applied linguist Alastair Pennycook takes a step further and advocates for a *translingual activism*.[32] If the monolingual monolith is a boundary stone, then speaking boundlessly is an act of resistance. We are *talking back* to the monolith with a fluid language that challenges and erodes the rigidity of linguistic purism and cultural nativism.

Enabling translanguaging practices is particularly crucial in the English as a foreign language classroom. Disentangling formal education from its historical bounds would enable us to start decolonising our languaging lives.

Deborah tells me how, when she teaches, she is now consciously choosing not to perpetuate the language estrangement we once experienced. She sees language education as enabling her students to speak more closely to what they truly mean and, when doing so, grammar and code-mixing should not be their primary concerns. She makes a rule to mark her students' work only with ticks and question marks, and never with the written mark of a cross.

'You want them to use the language and say what they think,' Deborah explains. 'So first of all, they need to know that there's nothing wrong with them expressing their thoughts.'

It is but a small change to the pedagogy, but it contributes significantly to lifting the profound barriers between our languages. Students no longer need to wait to speak, and they can say what they mean by choosing freely from all the words they have in their repertoire. It is only when we can utter an English word without feeling estranged from it that we can start claiming ownership over the language, and close the alienating distance between us and our in-between culture.

The change is also happening beyond the education space. A new generation of bilingual writers from Hong Kong has broken the alienating silence by claiming ownership over the English language with their works. In her Hong Kong memoir, *The Impossible City*, writer and journalist Karen Cheung interlaces her English narrative with epigraphs, lyrics, and catchphrases in Cantonese to create a unique, contrapuntal musicality that underscores the hybridity of the city she grew up in. Poet Tim Tim Cheng's English poems read like an iridescence with her use of deconstructed logograms, Cantonese puns, and loan translations, offering a kaleidoscopic view of the translingual realm in which she dwells.

The waves promise to weather any rigidity away, given enough time. By submerging ourselves in the ebb and flow of our multilingualism, we – as teachers, writers, learners, and speakers of English as a foreign language – are eroding the monolingual monolith with each undulating utterance.

There's no speaking it right. There's no speaking it wrong. So long as we're speaking still, a boundless language is coming into being word by word.

Chapter 2
Feels Translated: On Silence, Selfhood, and Belonging

WORDS AND WORLDS

It was an ordinary mid-May evening in 2024 in London. I was having dinner with my Hong Kong friends, Karen and Sze Pui, at a pasta joint near Old Street. Our friendship began over a decade ago when we were still in university: we were part of a close-knit cohort of a small programme, and bonded over our shared girlhood memories of CLAMP's manga and Taiwanese television and cinema.

We splurged on a bottle of wine that evening, for it had become a special occasion for us to simply be together. In Hong Kong, thanks to how compact the city is, getting together is never too big of a challenge – so long as one is willing to make the time. In recent years, however, Hongkongers have been adapting to being separated from their families and friends by long distances. Following a new wave of mass emigration from Hong Kong since 2019, many Hongkongers are now scattered across the world. Karen is currently still based in Hong Kong but visits London regularly. Sze Pui has moved to London for good, with her parents settling down in Hampshire. As for me, I'm oscillating between the life I'm making for myself in London, and the life I get to spend with my mother in Hong Kong.

The three of us, finally reunited over the dinner table, sat by the window. It was warm and cozy in the restaurant, but the streets outside were getting drenched. *Is May supposed to feel like this?* we asked each other in disbelief as we stared into the cold London rain. We forgot that we were no longer in the subtropics, and it was not the late spring that we used to know.

Karen asked how we were getting on.

Sze Pui, who had the perceptive articulateness of a litigator, had changed careers since she moved to the UK, and took up a new job as a law reporter. She confessed that she found herself at a loss for words sometimes in the office, pondering if the forthrightness in her usual professional vernacular might be read as bluntness in the unfamiliar jurisdiction of a new cultural register. I told Karen a joke I didn't get to tell from earlier, when I went to the pub with some new friends. It was a remark which I thought would have made a witty comeback but decided against sharing at the time, knowing from trial and error that the cultural references and wordplay that made up my sense of humour might not withstand its translation into English.

Much to my belated delight, it did give Karen a hearty laugh.

We shared with each other the recent chaos of language we experienced via what can only be described as another chaos of language. We were trying to catch up with each other too eagerly on multiple things at the same time, and we ended up often speaking over each other in our own personal mixes of Cantonese and English.

Our language mishmash was an absolute mess, one that our teachers would have frowned upon. Unapologetically undesirable, unsophisticated, and vulgar, it was nonetheless the best way to help us understand each other in such a brief reunion.

The evening flew by. Still drunk on the joy of finally seeing each other, we stepped into the cold rain as the restaurant closed for the night. Huddling up under the canopy at the door, I asked Karen and Sze Pui, 你點返屋企 (nei5 dim2 faan1 uk1 kei2) – *how are you getting home?*

Before the girls could answer, the question hit me with an odd sense of contradiction.

It felt both familiar and strange at the same time. It was a standard question to end our gatherings, one that we had asked each other numerous times before; but it had meant something different in the past.

In another time-space, the question used to precede Sze Pui running to catch the last bus back to her family home in Yuen Long, Karen hailing a taxi to her place up those haunted, hilly streets in Sheung Wan, and me taking a stroll across Causeway Bay under the neon lights to get to my small flat at the other side of the Hong Kong Victoria Park.

But we had since moved out of those homes and the bodily memories that guided our past directions. The question of home was now a metalinguistic moment with new ambiguities, and a secret wordplay understandable only by those who had also been displaced.

你點返屋企? asked the ones who had taken the fixed definition of home for granted for too long, sheltered by the privilege of what was once a settled life.

Perhaps it has always been a complex question that prompts more questions than answers.

Could homes be temporary, such that Karen could call the guest room in Highgate she was staying in her 屋企? In a quest for a sense of stability, I moved four times in the span of two years, first across three cities, then up and down the two banks of the River Thames. Do I get to call all these places I sojourned *home*, so long as I longed for permanence? Is it greedy of me to try to claim both Hong Kong and London as my *uk kei* at the same time? And for Sze Pui, where a decision to stay has been made, will a permanent address finally start to make her feel at home when she roams the streets of London?

At the end of the day, even though the words bear the same meaning, will the English *home* be able and willing to bear the weight of the joys, woes, and memories of our Cantonese *uk kei*?

Home has no easy answer – for it is more than just a roof over our heads; it is also a feeling.

It is the feeling of protection, a refuge where you can watch the typhoon safely from behind thick windows with your cat purring on your lap. It is a reassurance, in the form of a place or a people, holding each other close against the unsettling unpredictability of this world. It is a freedom to wander, to stroll through the alleys and paths without fear, even as the last lights of the city switch off. It is also the sense of one's roots, the place from which we grow and branch into the world, as well as the very stem through which we find our way back.

This feeling of being at home, as sociologist Nira Yuval-Davis suggests, is an emotional or ontological attachment; in other words, home is a sense of belonging.[33]

So we find our way home, as we negotiate the terms of how we belong to each other. People have done it in various ways. Some take belonging as a question of food, asked and answered in the aromas, tastes, and colours that bring back the deepest and fondest childhood memories. Some seek their belonging in fashion, making intimate cultural connections in the touch of materials and the silhouettes made on the body. Some find their belonging in their heritage, the folklores and rites that are passed down through generations, in the steadfastness of collective memories against the ferocious turning of time.

As for me, in my two tongues, the question of belonging manifests itself in translation.

Philosopher Paul Ricoeur sees translation as having a double duty, both internal and external: it is at once a task of translating oneself to oneself, and that of translating oneself to others.[34] In this sense, we are constantly translating between the heart and the world. If *who we are* is a story that we repeatedly tell ourselves and others, prior to displacement, we often take ourselves to be an original text where the alignment between our self-understanding and our perceived identity is taken as a given. We feel at home in this text, having a sense of control over our own narrative and a mastery over the words that connect ourselves with others.

A translation problem arises when we move home. As we move from one physical, affective, and linguistic place to another, we become transposed, disoriented, unsettled. Migration is thus a rupture: it breaks apart the presumed connection between the heart and the world, compelling us to re-consider who we are and where we belong, in search of a renewed congruence between the in and the out.

Migration makes us conscious of the need to translate.

We are made in language, and we dwell in language. To move home, near or far, always means making choices. We pack up our most precious belongings and let go of what we can't hold on to. Keep the photo albums and our mothers' recipe books, but perhaps not the timeworn posters on the walls or letters from past lovers. In the same manner, as we move from one language to another and speak again, we can only pick the words we cherish the best and leave the rest behind. When explaining ourselves, we choose among our many names and nicknames, our favourite poems and proverbs. We can't translate them all, and can only translate as closely as we can.

We move across the world and step into the unknown, carrying with us a carefully curated array of belongings and words, each find is a remnant of dismantled homes and narratives that once made us who we were. From there, using what we have left and what we can find, we rebuild our homes brick by brick, as we reconstruct our identities word by word.

After our displacement, we no longer have full control over the words we utter. Post-rupture, as we translate from the heart into the world, the story of who we are could be understood and welcomed, or it could be misread and distorted.

Translation, like migration, is therefore a bittersweet process of lost and found. In our quest for a new self and a new home, we seek a bona fide re-presentation of our selfhood and our belonging, as we try to reiterate our stories as faithfully as possible.

RUPTURE AND RECOVERY

It was back in summer 2023: a month or two after I moved to London, I injured my ankle in an accident and couldn't walk for weeks.

I was never a mindful enough walker, for I had never learnt to mind my steps. Being born in a small city and raised in the same neighbourhoods meant I rarely needed to check my directions or reconfirm my route. Most of the time, I could just rely on my bodily memory to take me from home to school or from work to gym, from one familiar place to another. For too long in my life, I thought 我瞇埋眼都識路 (ngo5 mei1 maai4 ngaan5 dou1 sik1 lou6) – *I knew my way even with my eyes closed*.

But then I moved from Hong Kong to the UK in 2022, or – in the jargon of those motivational social media accounts – *I pushed myself out of my comfort zone*.

That sense of control I had over my directions quickly dissipated over the six thousand miles that I travelled.

It didn't take me long to realise I didn't in fact know my way. I only thought I did because of the many people around me who were ready to catch me whenever I tripped. Perhaps I was never the fittest person to leave my comfort zone, but by the time I realised this, I was already in an extended process of moving homes. From Hong Kong to Oxford and on to London, and from south of the river to the north, I kept adjusting to new environments in the two years that followed. After each move, I always felt I had lost my routine: the important habits that gave me stability and support. Thereafter, I always suffered from a severe sense of alienation. I was so homesick, but I didn't even know where home was or would be. Much like all the moving boxes I never managed to unpack in time, I felt all over the place.

A month or two after moving into this place in which I'm currently writing, I felt the desperate need to rebuild a routine just to confront my irrational fear of stepping out of the flat. When a friend asked me to join her in a Tanztheater summer course at a dance studio nearby, I said yes. *I could use the walk to familiarise myself with the new neighbourhood*, I thought. *It'd be good exposure therapy.*

As things transpired, the walk was probably not the best idea at the time.

I was too disoriented by the intense moving I had just gone through. Google Maps was acting up. It was a rainy day. Blaming everything else but my own absentmindedness, I failed to notice a gap in the pavement and fell over.

What followed was a loud *pop* sound, and an ankle that got twisted into a strange angle. Right away, I registered that it was a medical emergency, the last thing I needed when I was already struggling in a new place.

I was immediately immobilised and was blacking out from the pain. Sitting down by the pavement, I took out my phone in panic.

I need help, I told myself.

I didn't call 999. Nor did I ring up my partner who was my emergency contact. Instead, in a moment of utmost bewilderment, I took on to Google intuitively to look for the help I most desperately needed.

I searched: how do I say 扭傷 (nau2 soeng1), *twisted injury*, in English?

I have always considered myself quite articulate when it comes to my bodily feelings. Partly it was because I was quite frail as a child; it was a result of 久病成醫 (gau2 beng6 sing4 ji1), *becoming a doctor from my own sickliness*. It was also because of my late father. He was training to become a traditional Chinese medicine doctor in China until he was forced to give up his education during the Cultural Revolution, and eventually emigrated to Hong Kong. In our years together, I picked up from him a variety of words to describe my pains and illnesses. Placing his fingers on my pulse for a diagnosis, he would refer to my palpitations as 心悸 (sam1 gwai3) *heart fright*, insomnia as 肝鬱 (gon1 wat1) *liver stagnation*, colds and flu as 風邪入侵 (fung1 ce4 jap6 cam1) *wind malice infringement*. Then he would make me the herbal teas that were pungently bitter, yet would never fail to make me feel better than Xanax or melatonin or paracetamol.

Yet my father 醫不自醫 (ji1 bat1 zi6 ji1)– *was a doctor but couldn't treat himself*. I lost him to cancer years ago. Still, I have him in my Cantonese memories, and I know how to ask him for help. I can picture how he would kneel in front of me by the pavement and place my foot on his lap. He would move my ankle gently, testing 通唔通 (tung1 m4 tung1), *passing through or not*, and ask me 痛唔痛, *painful or not* (tung3 m4 tung3). Finally, he would assure me that I am going to be okay. 冇傷及筋骨 (mou5 soeng1 kap6 gan1 gwat1), *the injury didn't reach the tendons and bones,* he would say.

In Cantonese, I know I'm going to be okay. It is a language I speak so well that I can articulate the nuances in my pains. I'm fluent in voicing my vulnerabilities out loud. In English, however, none of my comfort words would come to my rescue. It is perhaps a cliché to say that one feels particularly lonely and helpless when one falls sick in an unfamiliar land, but what I had was exactly that feeling, just manifested in language.

You, and only you, can feel the piercing pain or dull ache under your skin. You fear that for as long as you can't communicate your vulnerabilities across, the pain will stay within your bodily bounds, and no one will ever understand.

You feel this is a language in which you can't cry for help.

Psychoanalysts believe that our language begins in the very need to cry for help.[35] All lives begin in a plenitude: when we are still in the womb, or when we are still unknowing infants, we live in an abundant silence that lacks nothing. There, we are inseperable from our caregivers, and all our needs are already provided for before we even have to ask for them. Then we go through our first loss: we are born and separated from our mothers. We grow and come to realise that we are on our own now, no longer one with our mother figures. We experience what we lack, and we begin to desire.

In this first trauma of separation, we as infants realise we must now cry to get what we need. Then we start to whimper and babble, and eventually, we speak. As professor of philosophy Noëlle McAfee puts it, 'The story is a sad one, but it is the story of how human beings create civilization. We learn language and its accompanying arts as a kind of compensation for what we must all lose: being embraced by our mother's body.'[36]

It is therefore in our futile attempt to return to the serene silence of our mother's all-encompassing embrace that we acquire language, and it is in this language made in the ruptures of separation and loss that we come into being.

Rupture it was. When I eventually got to the A&E, I was told my ligament was partially torn.

A *ligament* – a word I had to look up in the dictionary afterwards – is the tissue of stability and support. Uncanny, but it is an apt metaphor for the state of migration. To move into a realm of unknown, and to be parted with familiar territories, is very much like navigating a strange city with a torn ligament. You lose the privilege to be reckless and must now watch every step you take. You limp because you fear hurting yourself. You slow yourself down to avoid triggering the pain.

A torn ligament is also by definition an injury from the sudden impact of movement. The rupture may be abrupt, taking only seconds, but the recovery process could be long.

In my first physiotherapy session, I was asked what my recovery goals were. I was confused this was even a question. *Of course I wanted to be able to walk again, in the exact same way as before.*

This is how we often think of a recovery: being restored to the original state, as if there had never been any change in the first place. Getting well should mean becoming the same person again. When we finally recover from a trauma, we should walk and talk and dance and laugh exactly as we did before.

This definition of recovery is not unlike what is conventionally understood as a good translation of a text. If we think of ourselves as a text, each telling a unique story of our identity and our belonging, then we are all translating our own narratives whenever we migrate. Despite the displacement of language and culture, we often expect the translated text to speak as fluently as before. To do so, the translator must strive to write in an invisible hand and conceal their existence when they orchestrate the transfer of words. As American translator Lawrence Venuti describes, it is commonly believed that the best translation should appear as if it were the original, under an illusion of transparency of fluent discourse.[37]

From word to word, we hide the fact that a conductor intervenes in the meaning-exchange between our hearts and our worlds. With every step, we mask our limping, pretending that our wound doesn't hurt.

As I have found out, however, concealing changes in life is very difficult.

In the months following the rupture, I slowly learnt to walk again. First with the help of a pair of crutches, then with endless patience, hoping to regain my balance. Meanwhile, I struggled to adapt to a new way of speaking about vulnerabilities. As I went through the therapy process, I had to gradually translate my repertoire of ailments into English. When I first started, I spoke like a child. With a limited vocabulary around pain, I was clumsy when describing to my physiotherapist how I felt, and relied on imprecise metaphors. *The branch is unwilling to bend*, I would say, when explaining why I couldn't lift my heel properly when I walked. Another time, out of desperation, I referred to the nagging ache hidden in the side of my foot as *the pea under the mattresses*. It was as if I was limping also in the English language, reminiscing the control and balance I had between my two tongues.

Whatever definition we take for our recovery, one thing is for sure – it is never a linear process.

At some point, when the rehabilitation exercises felt impossibly monotonous, I became overwhelmed by anxiety. What else could I possibly do to perfect my recovery and find that flawless translation that would allow me to walk in the same stride and talk with the same confidence again? Would I ever be able to restore myself to who I once was, to feel at home in my own skin like before?

How do we carry on with our lives, in the aftermath of displacement and rupture?

TRANSLATION AND TRANSCENDENCE

After a long convalescence, spring arrived again.

Over the months, I established a new routine of physiotherapy sessions, stretching exercises, and massages before bed. In those new habits, I stopped consciously thinking about my wound all the time; and in this intermittent forgetfulness, I slowly adapted to a different pace of life.

It was approaching the end of March. The sun rose earlier each day, pushing daylight into the dark. The clock was about to go forward, and London and Hong Kong would once again be brought one hour closer to each other.

One of the biggest differences between Hong Kong and London is in how the cities experience the seasons. In Hong Kong, the dominant season is summer, and in-between seasons like spring and autumn are brief and subtle. In London, I can easily tell the seasons apart. My favourite tree in my current neighbourhood, a maple at the corner of a stone walk, sends the clearest seasonal messages with leaves that change colour, shed, and regrow.

London is also where when I first experienced, without any moderation by the subtropical climate, the ancient wisdom of 節氣 (zit3 hei3). 節氣 refers to the *solar terms* by which the traditional lunisolar calendar names twenty-four natural phenomena in the seasonal cycles. When 白露 (baak6 lou6), *White Dew*, crystalises in the morning in September, for instance, the weather starts to get dry and cold. When winter frost ceases in early March and small bugs reappear from the soil, the year returns to 驚蟄 (ging1 zik6), *Dormant Awakening*.

Consoled by the unfailing seasonal changes, I embraced the arrival of yet another 春分 (ceon1 fan1), *Spring Equinox*, when I would mourn my father's passing.

My father passed away in the last days of March in 2016, during a subtropical spring. Enough time has lapsed for me to stop consciously thinking about this loss all the time. Occasionally, when life gets busy enough, I even forget about the Equinox altogether. But that March, knowing that I was particularly vulnerable in an injured body and in an unfamiliar city, I did the responsible grown-up thing that the internet advised me to do.

I talked to a counsellor.

Unlike my wonky ankle, this was not a new wound. It was a wound that I had become quite experienced in handling. Over the years, I had stopped shying away from the fact that I had lost a parent. I kept track of my feelings. I had even got a well-rehearsed, just-candid-enough narrative about the events, if anybody ever asked.

I thought I had become quite fluent in this loss, but then, for the first time, I mourned in translation.

Looking at the kind stranger that was my new counsellor, I told her the story, this time in English. She told me to take my time, and I did. In front of her, I couldn't resort to my all-too-familiar narrative of loss in Cantonese; I had to gather my thoughts and translate my words, before I could begin to grieve in a language that I didn't share with my father, about the moments I shared with him.

I recounted how baffled I always felt about his capricious temperament. I described an early adulthood spent in caregiving, the constant fear about the eventuality, and the exhaustion of spending hours waiting outside operating theatres. I talked about that phone call from the hospital, the one that I had been dreading for years, that early morning in March. I recalled how I stood outside the ward, and the doctor delivered a long, scientific speech about the stopping of the heart.

In a less familiar tongue, I told a familiar story, and in the process, the old story changed.

In my translation of one of the most difficult narratives in life, I mourned in a second language with a limited emotional vocabulary and rudimentary metaphors. But exactly because I distanced myself from my most familiar words – the words that my father gave me – it hit differently.

I had felt a lot of things before, whenever I told people my story with my father – sad, indifferent, regretful, angry, grateful, joyous, brave.

This time, when I talked about my father in English, I felt safe.

I felt safe because I didn't have to worry that he might hear me cry and learn that I was hurt. I felt safe because I could now use words independent from him to describe him, and it didn't feel as if I was being immature and badmouthing him when I recounted my sorrow and rage.

I felt safe because in translation, I finally felt how I had changed. Across the yawning space that translation had opened up, I could finally see my trauma properly: it was no longer bleeding as I first knew it. Instead, with the passage of time, a scab had formed and fallen off my wound, turning it into a soft scar.

I have spent years trying to recover from this injury, and I still have not been fully restored. Maybe I will never be. However, rather than seeing this as a failure to move on, I now see how the changes in life have made a visible mark on me, as a new part of my own skin and flesh, born delicately out of a past trauma.

A scar is, after all, evidence of our ability to heal.

Translation is also a process of healing.

An art psychotherapist friend of mine once shared an analogy to describe the healing distance created by translation: she compares it to a snow globe.[38] It is as if I have placed my past joys and woes into a snow globe, and reappreciating the scene as a person who has changed and grown.

Her generous words lead me to a gentler perspective of the emotional politics of bilingualism. Recalling Ngũgĩ wa Thiong'o's words, as a non-native speaker of English, I have been *seeing myself from outside myself as if I am another self*,[39] but if I shift my position from translation-as-rupture to that of translation-as-healing, I am no longer forced into this perspective by colonial alienation;

rather, I am willingly doing so through a beautiful snow globe held firmly in my own hands.

At the distance so created, it gives me the time and space to understand and see things in a more forgiving light. If change is inevitable, then I can also change my relationship to the traumatic event – be it the loss of a loved one, a home, or a familiar language.

Paul Ricoeur understands translation in the same vein. In his philosophy, translation is understood broadly as the interpretative pursuit of a meaningful whole with others. He also sees translation as a site for peacemaking. Richard Kearney summarises Ricoeur's view: 'It is only when we translate our own wounds into the language of strangers and retranslate the wounds of strangers into our own language that healing and reconciliation can take place.'[40]

I had always thought of my mother tongue as the original that I must translate myself from, the ideal eloquence I must restore myself to, but I would have never experienced the nuances in the four seasons, or found the opportunity to tell my family story differently, if there had never been a distance created by migration and translation.

In my mother tongue, in the position of home that I had taken for granted, all these newfound parts of me would have never existed. 'Like all intimacies, the intimacy between one and one's mother tongue can be comforting and irreplaceable,' writes Yiyun Li, 'yet it can also demand more than what one is willing to give, or more than one is capable of giving.'[41]

Perhaps my mother tongue has instilled in me an inhibition, a self-restraint, an aversion to change. There are all these things that I can't talk about freely in Cantonese, and one of them is death. We skip the fourth floors in buildings because 四 (sei3), *four*, is almost homophonous with 死 (sei2), *death*. We use euphemisms to describe the things surrounding it: a funeral parlour is 長生店 (coeng4 sang1 dim3), *longevity shop*; a will is 平安紙 (ping4 on1 zi2), *peace paper*. And when we send our condolences when the inevitable happens, we say 節哀 (zit3 oi1), *rein in your grief*.

It is in English, a language that I am not native to, that I am given the chance to translate a feeling long reined in in my heart into open words for the world. It is in the mother tongue of another person that I find the space to reconcile with myself and my most familiar language.

In translation, we make peace with ourselves through others.

We realise the original could likewise create conflicts, hurt, silences, and we realise the native language is not omnipotent. In her investigation of the history of the mother tongue, professor of German and Comparative Literature Yasemin Yildiz refuses to take the concept as a given. Instead, she defines *mother tongue* broadly as a language that relates to familial inheritance, social embeddedness, emotional attachment, personal identification, and linguistics competence.[42] Given its complex relation to the political and affective issues of kinship, society, and identity, Yildiz explains that the mother tongue could also become 'a site of alienation and disjuncture' that 'blocks from view the possibility of multiple, and even contradictory attachments, of desire for something unfamiliar and unrelated as well as the pleasure derived from new childhoods and new connections.'[43]

Translation, as such, frees us from monolithic, homogenous understandings of home, native language, culture, and nation-state. Together with migration, the act of translation expands our ideas of who we can be, and where we can belong.

A rupture is not only about loss and pain; it could also be a catalyst for growing *beyond*. The displacement from a familiar home, history, and culture can therefore also be a rite of passage through defamiliarisation. We break ourselves off from the otherwise naturalised everyday running of our language and our lives, such that we could find space to accommodate an expanded definition of our selves and our belonging.

It is through an injured body that I have stopped taking walking for granted and gained a new mindfulness in my stride. It is also through giving up my rehearsed narrative of loss that I have found new ways to grieve and to heal.

To translate is to reconcile. As individuals or a collective, we break our status quo such that the silence hidden among us could reveal itself as a force of change. We submit to it, trusting that it will transform us into a new meaningful whole that embraces more diverse lived experiences.

To recover is to renew. In this sense, in the progression of life or in translation, we can never be *the same as before*. As Walter Benjamin writes in 'The Translator's Task': 'Just as fragments of a vessel, in order to be fitted together, must correspond to each other in the tiniest details but need not resemble each other, so translation, instead of making itself resemble the meaning of the original, must lovingly, and in detail, fashion in its own language a counterpart to the original's mode of intention, in order to make both of them recognizable as fragments of a vessel, as fragments of a greater language.'[44]

Recalling the question I asked at the beginning of this chapter, how, then, should we translate *home* or 屋企 into this greater language?

I long for a translation that transcends. One that brings about a new understanding of home that is broad enough to house all our similarities and differences. Home that can be temporary or permanent, tidy or messy, present or past, singular or plural. Home that provides stability and support, and yet is also ready to welcome changes. Home to which you feel belonging, whether you're celebrating your wins or mourning for your losses.

In the greater language, as Paul Ricoeur calls it, home is a *linguistic hospitality* 'where the pleasure of dwelling in the other's language is balanced by the pleasure of receiving the foreign word at home, in one's own welcoming house.'[45] Home is, as such, the unfailing readiness to translate, and an ongoing openness to understand the others, the unknown.

Even if it means taking a risk.

Even if it means unfamiliarity.

Even if it means rupture.

Throughout this book, and especially in this chapter, I have taken a risk by punctuating an English narrative with Chinese words. In one way or another, I have translated them: into proper English, through loan translations, or in footnote explanations. With those Chinese words, I might have broken the fluency of this essay apart; but in this breaking, I'm trying to create linguistic hospitality between the fragments of our languages, and open up a new space in which we could both dwell. It is your patience as a reader and listener that has given me the homely space to think in Cantonese alongside English, in words that are both the original and the translated. I hope that, in return, my language has also expanded the meanings in yours, as we piece a transcendent home together in our words.

Chapter 3

Unspoken Lingua Franca: On Silence as a Common Language

SOFT SUSURRUS

Some goodbyes are better made over long conversations, ones that allow you to get to know each other all over again like never before.

The year was 2022, a season of departure in Hong Kong. The world was beginning to defrost, both from winter and the pandemic that had held the world still for two years. People started moving around again, and that included me and my friend, Julianne.

I had just handed in my notice to quit my job. With a one-way flight ticket and no concrete plans for the future, I was about to leave Hong Kong for Oxford, where I would study for a year before deciding my next steps. Having ever only lived in the city I called my birthplace, it was going to be my first big move in life.

Julianne, on the other hand, was no stranger to moving around. Born and raised in Norway to Shanghainese immigrant parents, Julianne had lived across Scandinavia and Asia since a young age. Having stayed in Hong Kong first to study and then to work and spend more time with her grandma in the past years, she was about to leave the city, hoping to find a new life and a new career elsewhere.

We met up for a farewell walk along Bowen Road, a leafy, meandering trail up in the hills that overlooked the skyscrapers over the Hong Kong Island. It was a breezy day, and the wind prodded our conversation towards all the other goodbyes we had recently exchanged with other people.

It was a quiet conversation. Our voices were muffled by the masks that still covered every single face in the city at the time; and we spoke slowly and intermittently, as we translated ourselves for each other.

While our friendship began in a comparative literature class on Hong Kong poetry, Julianne and I have completely different mother tongues. Mine is Cantonese, and hers is a mix of Shanghainese and Norwegian. Our connection is built in English as our shared second language. Our conversations are typically punctuated by many pauses: sometimes we take our time to disentangle a strange-yet-familiar word from the tip of our tongues; sometimes we speak in charades; sometimes we simply rely on each other to complete our own sentences.

It was in this usual, meandering process of meaning-making, in an English we pieced together through our many other tongues, that Julianne told me about saying goodbye to her eighty-year-old grandma.

Julianne's grandma, who had migrated from China to Hong Kong decades ago, told Julianne that she fully supported her move, despite feeling *so veq teq*.

'So veq teq?' I asked, unable to match the Shanghainese syllables with the Chinese words I acquired through Cantonese in my repertoire.

But Julianne couldn't find the English words to properly translate *so veq teq* either, so she took out her phone, and began looking for the corresponding written characters.

We sat down on a bench by the road and fell into silence. I tuned in to the soft susurrus of the trees as Julianne carefully retrieved from an online dictionary the hardest goodbye she had exchanged with the tenderest of hearts. It took us a while, but I knew it was worth the wait: something significant was forming itself between our languages.

Then Julianne found it. *So veq teq*, when captured from the heart and put into writing, revealed itself as 捨勿得.

I recognised it immediately – my own mother had told me the same thing.

It is one of the most poignant phrases in Chinese, despite the differences in pronunciation and syntax among varieties of the language. In Shanghainese, *so veq teq* should be pronounced like the soft and swift fluttering of a butterfly's wings. Whereas in Cantonese, we say 唔捨得 (m4 se2 dak1), as if one is humming and musing about the butterfly's imminent departure.

Despite the different utterances, they point to the same meaning. 勿 (veq) and 唔 (m4) are negators. 捨得 (so teq / se2 dak1) is an oxymoron made out of two words: 捨 means *to lose* or *to let go*, and 得 means *to own* or *to gain*.

Altogether, 捨得 means *a willingness to lose one's hold*.

When Julianne's grandma spoke of *so veq teq*, she was encapsulating in three simple words the mother's dilemma: the bittersweetness of letting a child go. It denoted a sense of already missing someone before parting with them, because they had been a core part of you. It also meant not having the heart to see someone leave, for they had dwelled deeply in your heart in the first place.

'Isn't that also why we're doing this now,' I told Julianne as we gathered our coats from the bench, getting ready to carry on winding through Bowen Road.

'唔捨得大家,‡‡ so pausing every now and then for this moment to last longer.'

---

‡‡ m4 se2 dak1 daai6 gaa1, *unwilling to let go of each other*.

I left Hong Kong not long after. In the two years that followed, I moved across cities and riverbanks, trying to find new homes. I also had many conversations over many long walks with strangers, trying to make new connections.

Over this process of getting to know new places and new people, I slowly reflected on that quiet tête-à-tête I shared with Julianne. Its significance lied not only in what we said, but also in how we paused for each other.

Those pauses were pregnant with meaning that was deeper than any one single language could capture and flowing only in the interstices between our utterances. Those were still points in our conversations, or to borrow Paul Ricoeur's conceptualisation, *intermittent untranslatability*. We were unable to explain *so veq teq* adequately in English despite it being a shared second language, because the cultural and linguistic heterogeneity in the phrase resisted its own translation into another semantic field and syntax.[46] To communicate the feelings represented by that short Chinese phrase, as such, we had no choice but to meander, like the very footpath we were walking on.

For polyglots like Julianne and me to understand each other, there is no shortcut. Where a life is lived across cultures, we must move through languages to speak of it. We must also accept that there will be detours, in the form of occasional pauses and intermittent untranslatability, on our way to find mutuality in words. For this reason, the silent moments in our speech are not disruptions; instead, they are the preconditions to our connection.

I think of the dear strangers I met in the UK who eventually turned into my friends. There is Lara, who has lived a life in Düsseldorf and The Hague before we encountered each other on our first day in Oxford. We grew close to each other over our walks along the canal that connected our dormitory rooms. Lara is a fast walker, and I often have to jog to catch up with her, but in our conversations, we have always taken our time. If we had never slowed down and embraced the intermittent silences between us, we would never have found out that we share the same favourite words in our respective mother tongues: *tenderness* is *die Zärtlichkeit* is 溫柔 (wan1 jau4); *tree* is *der Baum* is 樹 (syu6); *sunshine* is *der Sonnenschein* is 陽光 (joeng4 gwong1).

There is also Andrea, who came all the way from Peru such that we could meet in our master's course and experience our first British winter together. We were both used to mild winters growing up, and struggled to adjust to the cold. As snow fell and melted over the winter months, Andrea gradually translated her feelings of loneliness from Spanish into a mix of silences, hugs, and English and trusted them with me, making me realise that I wasn't alone in my longing for the subtropical warmth back home. In the words I rummaged out of my repertoire, I told Andrea perhaps we could find solace in knowing that even when the winter nights felt impossibly long, the summer sun would always be shining over either Hong Kong or Lima.

These are friendships from different mother tongues, founded upon the fortuitous convergence of our languaging lives. While English as a common language has enabled me to exchange my life stories with these kindred spirits, my bond with them is rooted in the shared silences in our conversations, when we pause from our narratives and take the time to search for a word, translate a feeling, allegorise an experience. It is in those still points in our communications that we catch a first glimpse of how far we have each journeyed across languages and cultures to arrive at the moment where we are present for each other.

So it is not in our eventual utterances, but in the meaningful silences preceding our speech, that we begin building a connection.

Between us, reciprocity is found not only in language, but also in the unspoken. It is our mutual appreciation of each other's unsung courage in moving away from the familiar and opening ourselves up to the unknown. It is the reassurance that whenever one of us goes into a still point mid-conversation, we already know that we are not being passive or disengaged, but rather we are eagerly looking for the best words in our complex repertoires to bring us closer to each other. It is also a sense of relief and solidarity, like bumping into a fellow traveller at a crossroads, who can empathise with the displacement you have been through, the challenges and inspirations you experienced in your winding journey, and your longing for home.

Through all these tacit understandings, we find a new sense of home in our shared unhomeliness. We also find a new way to speak to each other in a lingua franca made from our shared silences.

Lingua franca, a term that was historically used to describe a pidgin developed by traders in the eastern Mediterranean, now refers to the language used for communication between people who speak different languages. It is a malleable and diverse concept, full of radical potential. Where our conventional understanding of language has been monolithic, tangled up in cultural nativism and linguistic purism, the concept of lingua franca intervenes in those intertwining chains as a pair of attentive hands that patiently unties the language knots. By putting its emphasis on *communication*, a lingua franca is a language of humility and hospitality, a friend that is keen to know you. It imposes no fixed fluency standard or rigid grammar rules on the people who choose to adopt it; rather, it welcomes its speaker with open arms, ready to be shaped and reshaped to suit one's needs. A lingua franca is also an active listener. It appreciates that you may have come from a different culture, and are weary in your quest, so you might not be as outspoken or articulate as you used to be. It wants to understand your story anyway, even if told non-verbally. When your vocabulary runs out, the lingua franca encourages metaphors, gestures, facial expressions. For as long as you would like to share, it will adapt and accommodate.

So, when we speak to each other with a tacit understanding of our intercultural and interlingual differences, the English we speak breaks free from the grip the native speaker phantom has on us. As we speak, we reconceptualise and claim ownership over our English as a lingua franca.

Scholars in critical language education see the power of English as a Lingua Franca, or what they call ELF for short, in transforming our cultural discourse. They see ELF as 'open, unfinalisable, dynamic, contingent, fragmented, variable and inseparable from context', the means through which we could move away from rigid nativist standards, and towards a more complex and fluid understanding of language.[47]

Since we are made in language, if we reframe the very modalities by which we feel, think, and live from the monolithic native tongue into the heterogenous lingua franca, it could also transform the way we see ourselves and others.

It has transformed my relationship to language and silence. If I am to condense this book into a couple of sentences, this narrative begins in an outcry: *English has silenced me*. In this position, I put English as the active subject, the do-er, and myself as the passive object, the done-to. Silence is imposed on me, and I have no control over it; it unsettles my languaging self, and disempowers my speech. However, if we consider the possibility of any language to be a lingua franca, then silence is part of how I communicate. This will enable me to now say, in revelation, *I speak in English and silence*. The English language, reframed this way as a lingua franca, now hands the agency over to me. I claim my ownership over it, as I also reclaim my silence.

Importantly, this freedom is not a new invention; it is just a rediscovery. Like every other language in this world, English has always been inherently heterogenous. Russian philosopher and literary critic Mikhail Bakhtin calls the internal diversity of language *heteroglossia*. As Bakhtin writes in 'Discourse in the Novel', any single language can be internally stratified into 'social dialects, characteristic group behavior, professional jargons, generic languages, languages of generations and age groups, tendentious languages, languages of the authorities, of various circles and of passing fashions, languages that serve the specific sociopolitical purposes of the day, even of the hour.'[48]

As such, we are all heteroglossic speakers. If I could push this concept a step further, even if we only speak one language, we are still polyglots in a broad sense. For we are always translating as we speak, between our hearts and our worlds, and between ourselves and others. As long as we are speaking to reach a mutual understanding with others, we are constantly deciding the best modalities to communicate and reconcile our differences. Even in our mother tongues, we are still always translanguaging, switching among our various means of meaning-making.

The lingua franca sees no difference between those who speak a language natively and those who has only acquired the words later. It is a great equaliser: the unhomeliness, alienation, or grief experienced by those travelling into a foreign tongue could resonate with those who are native to that language but switch to a new stratification, as Bakhtin suggests, within their own tongue. Likewise, the freedom, wonder, and solace that speakers find when they dwell in a foreign language could also be rediscovered in a reconceptualised mother tongue. This is all possible, as long as we choose to communicate.

Make silence our new lingua franca. Take a pause from our ceaseless conversations. Insert still points into our ongoing narratives. Disrupt the homogenous definition of our lives and cultures and histories with a quiet moment.

When we shut our mouths and begin to tune into the world beyond us, it can feel terribly like losing at first, as if we are losing our hold on our narratives.

If it does, then we are doing the right thing.

For if we recall the oxymoronic wisdom of 捨得, we must *lose* before we *gain*. It is only when we let go of the given voice and choose silence that we begin to communicate in a way that goes deeper than any named language.

The world is loud, filled to the brim with utterances, arguments, reasonings, narratives, and discourses that we have long taken without question. Silence stands as a radical alternative to this worldly, normative clamour: it slows us down, quiets our conditioned thinking, and frees up a space in which we can now tune into all the unheard possibilities.

As Mary Oliver reminds us in her poem 'Praying',

> . . . this isn't
> a contest but the doorway
> into thanks, and a silence in which
> another voice may speak.[49]

Let words fail us, as they must, for us to find the ways to truly speak to ourselves and others.

BEYOND THE SOUND

In the essay where Audre Lorde made the famous feminist cri de coeur, 'your silence will not protect you', she also urged for 'the transformation of silence into language and action'.[50] It was the 1970s. Speaking up against racism in the context, Lorde was rightfully deeming silence as fear, censure, annihilation, even tyranny. By transforming silence, Lorde meant breaking and replacing it with activism.

Throughout this book, we have looked at silence differently – as an intriguing paradox. In line with Lorde's perspective, we have considered the ways in which silence could mean powerlessness; but we have equally explored how we could reclaim silence as empowerment. Now that I am about to bring this book to a close, I would like to take one more linguistic risk and open Lorde's words up for a different interpretation with the pragmatic ambiguities inherent in the phrase.

What alternative meaning could 'the transformation of silence into language and action' bring?

As Lorde argued elsewhere in the same essay, the thing that 'makes us most vulnerable is that which also is the source of our greatest strength.'[51] Then why can't we also see silence as where we draw our strength? We have explored how it is possible to redeem silence as becoming, as connection, as home. Speaking in silence as a lingua franca, we can now reinterpret 'the transformation of silence into language and action' not as a simple rejection of silence, but the adaption of the same into a quiet way to act.

Instead of replacing silence by language and action, in our context, we can see silence *as* language and action. When we are engaging in silence, it means we are articulating the unknown, welcoming subdued ways of life, and hearing beyond familiar notes.

Taking this as a point of departure, how can silence transform us as individuals? How can silence reimagine the way we belong to each other?

In search of an answer, I sought out the work of inspiring people I came across as I wandered around oscillating between my selves as a Hongkonger and a Londoner, a sojourner and a dweller, a friend and a stranger.

Some people, for instance, are building silence into a holding space.

In the summer of 2024, I volunteered at the Migration Museum at its temporary home at the Lewisham Shopping Centre in South London.

I first heard about the Migration Museum from a friend studying at Goldsmiths, a university nearby, who was going on a journey of figuring out her identity as a foreigner in the UK. I only paid my first visit to the Museum a few months later by chance. I was passing by the area, and noticed that I was in front of the Museum my friend had been talking about with so much enthusiasm. It was an exhibition space located right at the centre of a bustling shopping mall, at the heart of its community's everyday lives.

I was planning to just quickly browse the exhibition before getting on with my day. But as soon as I walked into the museum space, I was greeted by a wall full of colourful paper circles, which the Museum called *story discs*, on which countless visitors to the Museum had written down their migration stories, and shared them with strangers like me.

I ended up staying much longer at the Museum than expected, reading through the story discs that day. Not long after, I returned as a volunteer.

In one of the workshops I helped in, the facilitator asked the participating primary school pupils to form a circle, and take one small step forward whenever they heard a statement that applied to them.

One step forward, *if your grandparents or parents have moved here from another country.*

One step forward, *if you or your friend have lived in a different country before.*

One step forward, *if you speak a language other than English, regardless of fluency.*

The circle came closer and closer, as the children eagerly took larger and larger steps, until it almost became a group hug.

Going around the circle, the children then shared their stories. Some had grandparents who were originally from Senegal; some had a childhood in Norway. Some spoke Portuguese at home; some had picked up a few everyday Japanese phrases from a cousin.

I ask Cym Henry, the learning and volunteer coordinator of the Migration Museum, about the many circles the Museum is building.[52]

'Whether it's a circle that a school group sits in, or the physical museum space, we're always making a welcoming space,' Cym tells me. 'A space that makes you and your story feel at home, by being part of something bigger.'

Cym notes that different people might prefer to engage with the physical and emotional space in different ways. As he describes in detail, among the communities he has worked with, some are more outspoken, while others prefer not to share their ideas aloud. Those who are ready to share a lot, and others who mention only a small part of their stories. Those whose stories are joyful and have a happy ending, and others who have traumatic experiences that are too painful to recount. There are also those who need to speak in a second language, through a speech impediment, or a learning disability.

'But none of these differences should be a problem. If I'm leading a session and I only hear the loudest voices, or the voices that really want to be heard, then it's my failing as a facilitator.'

Cym sees silence as an inclusive holding space that allows people to take their time to gather and share their thoughts in a way and at a pace they feel safe. This holding space, he emphasises, is underpinned by empathy and honesty and embraces all views, whether sad or happy, dramatic or mundane.

Silence as an action, in this way, means active listening. 'As a baseline,' Cym concludes. 'We want to hear from everyone.'

In this spirit of togetherness, some other people are adapting silence into a language of care.

Rose Tsui, who moved from Hong Kong to the UK in 2021, is the community and education manager at the Discover Children's Story Centre in Stratford.[53] Discover is a children's literature museum that celebrates a love for language, literature, and stories, and serves the children and their grown-ups in Newham, one of the most ethnically, culturally and linguistically diverse boroughs in London. The museum's mission is to create a safe space for children, carers, and parents in which they can find their communities.

When I visit Rose at her workplace, the museum has just transformed itself into a Monster Funfair based on Nadia Shireen's award-winning picture books. We follow a group of giggling four- or five-year-olds into the fairground by crawling through a dinosaur's laser maze.

'English isn't really my go-to language.' Rose tells

me in a soft voice that almost gets drowned out by the whimsical music playing in the background. 'But this has somewhat become an advantage for me at work. Many of the parents I'm working with are first-generation immigrants like me, and English isn't their most comfortable language either. I think our distances with the language has drawn us closer to each other.'

Rose goes on to share with me an example of the languaging scene in a recent workshop she organised, in which parents and carers from the local areas learnt to turn their lived experiences into stories for their children.

'No one uses slang, no one uses flowery language, no one cares about accents. We talk in simple English, at a very slow pace, with a lot of patience, a lot of metaphors, and most importantly, a lot of body language.'

Rose shows me some of the gestures the participants used, and I marvel at how many profound life stories can be told in a few silent movements. *Pregnancy* is your palms cupping over your belly. *Baby* is a cradling position, with your hands under the elbows, gently rocking side by side. *Happiness* is your arms extended out into the air longingly as if initiating a hug. *Separation* is pushing your hands abruptly away, as if abandoning an invisible attachment.

'Sometimes, it can be so hard to explain our histories and ourselves,' Rose tells me as she guides me past a wall painted with multi-coloured cartoon worms that represent jitters in the tummy.

'But silence will always be there to catch you, even when your life experience is too heavy for words to bear.'

I think this is exactly how we go beyond the sound and listen to the marginalised, the subdued, the unheard – through silence as a holding space, and as a language of care.

Following the examples of Cym and Rose, we can also transform silence into language and action as individuals by becoming silence-aware in our everyday lives.

We begin with a pause. Practise pausing whatever you are doing, wherever you are going, however you are conducting yourself. The pauses can be so small: take a sip from your glass mid-conversation, take off your headphones for a moment when the train goes into the tunnel, take a moment before you re-watch that familiar scene from your favourite film yet again. What a pause does is to defamiliarise you with your own life, and insert still points into the quotidian. As if we are translating between languages, a pause estranges us from the saturated meanings and normative habits of our minds, exposing us to what Paul Ricoeur calls the 'test of the foreign'.[54]

The pause slows you down. It delays the forming of a view, forcing you to hesitate, rendering your familiar feelings tentative. It is like inviting silence as an interlocutor into a routine conversation, such as the unthinking exchange of the customary greeting of *you alright?* or its Cantonese counterpart 食咗飯未? (sik6 zo2 faan6 mei6), *have you eaten yet.* It then opens you up for the surprise of what silence may actually have to say, about its happiness and its wrath, its fortunes and its suffering.

Philosopher Alia Al-Saji argues that hesitation interrupts the stereotyping ways of seeing that we have often taken without question. Hesitation, as such, is the necessary condition for an ethical way to see ourselves and others. In hesitation, we start encountering unanticipated differences, which in turn open the cultural discourse sedimented in us to transformation and critique.[55]

We then surrender the obsessive dream of an all-encompassing, self-sufficient language and narrative of who we are. As individuals and collectives, we realise not everything can be perfectly translated into that dominant and neat story about our society. We become aware that, in the translation from the hearts into the world, some hearts are often left out as misfits to uphold homogeneity. So we pause that totalising and short-circuiting narrative, and put silence in as placeholders, while questioning with hesitation each time the narrative attempts to draw itself too readily to a close.

We hear ourselves asking silently: *Is that all of us? Have we heard from everybody? Is our current language sufficient to carry the unwieldy weight of all our stories?*

This is when we tune into what philosopher Gemma Corradi Fiumara calls the 'inconclusive modesty of the listener'.[56]

The space left open by silence thus becomes the fertile ground in which new understandings and meanings, especially the ones previously pushed out to the margins unbeknownst to us, can emerge and diversify the language in which we dwell.

When listening becomes a collective habit, silence becomes a new tacit cultural understanding among us. We insistently listen beyond the sound, renegotiate the terms of our senses of belonging, and push the enunciative boundaries of our culture.

In so doing, we remake ourselves and dwell in a new unspoken language – one that allows us to get to know each other all over again like never before.

Epilogue: Departing for Home

As I conclude *Speak Still* with this final chapter, I re-read my initial draft of the prologue. It felt like a re-encounter.

The prologue was originally written as a short, one-thousand-word piece for a creative writing course. For the many reasons I confessed earlier, I had never done much creative writing in English before; and even when I managed to write something, in verse or in prose, I had often felt too embarrassed to share my words.

Over the first few weeks of the writing course, I did more apologising than actual writing. A non-exhaustive list of the things I apologised for: sharing only fragmented thoughts instead of a coherent piece; submitting a lousy translation of a piece I originally wrote in Chinese; failing to write anything at all; getting all flustered and tongue-tied reading my own words aloud and explaining my own thoughts; not being quite like my usual self; my English.

My writing group was endlessly encouraging and supportive, but for that, I somehow also managed to apologise – *sorry, I'll stop saying sorry!*

It's a story that makes me blush even to recount, but in a way, it's also a rite of passage I had to go through. At one point, I trapped myself so deeply in that sense of speechlessness that I felt I had run out of all ideas and motivation to even put any word down onto the page.

But right when writing in English felt like an impossible task, I had a revelation.

If I knew nothing, then wouldn't it also mean I had at least some knowledge of what nothingness was?

That was how, with the almost metafictional hope of breaking that creative paralysis from within, I began writing about the impossibility of writing in English.

It was the autumn of 2023 (yes, still with a broken ankle and still crying about it). Over the following year, I started writing this book by looking ever so deeply into that impossibility. It involved a lot of talking to myself and others, as well as a lot of listening to myself and others, until all those conversations had ingrained in me a new habit and new perspective in the language, and until it no longer felt as impossible as before in the language to feel, to dream, and to create.

I think about the imagery of the sea and the voyage in the prologue. Now that we have arrived here at the other end, this book serves as an intimate testimony of that journey. It has been a journey of sailing out into the unknown on a quest for a voice, of reconciling with the silences in the sea, and most importantly, of discovering one of the many homecoming possibilities.

A rough idea of what this epilogue should look like was first scribbled down as a note in my phone in Kongish – a mix of Hong Kong English and Romanised Cantonese words. At the time, I was on a train towards the Heathrow Airport to catch an evening flight back to Hong Kong.

Moments before I made the notes, I received a message from my partner.

'Have you left home yet?' he asked.

It was just a quick, everyday question, but amidst the disorienting vastness that was the world, those simple words anchored my heart.

Yes, I have – I have left home for home.

It was now autumn 2024.

The writer and civil rights activist James Baldwin once had a quarrel with the English language because he felt it reflected none of his experience. But things changed when he started making the language his own. 'Perhaps the language was not my own because I had never attempted to use it, had only learned to imitate it,' he wrote in 1964. 'If this were so, then it might be made to bear the burden of my experience if I could find the stamina to challenge it, and me, to such a test.'[57]

I think a journey home is an ongoing test of one's stamina in returning to oneself. By attempting to use a language, and by challenging myself to make it bear the burden of my experience – which is the aggregate of all my hopes and woes and eloquence and speechlessness – I'm building the language into a new home.

A home that will house me and all my different selves, in the past, in the future, or in between.

When I asked myself the question of language and home when I first set off for the journey, I thought this book was written at the distance between me and the two tongues in which I dwell. That is still true, but if I'm to ask myself the question again, now knowing slightly more than nothing, I do have a more elaborate answer to give.

I have written this book at the distance of my bilingualism in order to close that distance.

In Chinese, when we end a letter to a loved one, we write 紙短情長 (zi2 dyun2 cing4 coeng4) – *the words run out, but the affection endures.* I must go now to board that flight, such that I can be close to you again. But do remember, even when I have reached the limit of my words, we are speaking still.

In silence, our longing for each other endures.

References

1. John M. Carroll, *A Concise History of Hong Kong*. Hong Kong University Press, 2006. pp10-13.
2. Jeannette Winterson, *Oranges Are Not The Only Fruit*. Vintage Books, 2014. p217.
3. Judith Butler, *Bodies that Matter: On the Discursive Limits of Sex*. Routledge, 2011. p171.
4. Judith Butler, *Gender Trouble: Feminism and the Subversion of Identity*. Routledge, 1999. p182.
5. Julia Kristeva, *The Portable Kristeva*. Edited by Kelly Oliver. Columbia University Press, 1997. p275.
6. Ibid.
7. Wisława Szymborska, 'The Three Oddest Words'. In *Map: Collected and Last Poems*, translated by Clare Cavanagh and Stanislaw Baranczak. Houghton Mifflin Harcourt, 2015. p328.
8. Michel Foucault, 'An Interview with Michel Foucault by Charles Ruas'. In *Death and the Labyrinth*, translated by Charles Ruas. Continuum, 2006. p179.
9. Richard Kearney, 'Introduction: Ricoeur's Philosophy of Translation'. In *On Translation*, by Paul Ricoeur, translated by Eileen Brennan. Routledge, 2006. pxix.
10. Cheryl Glenn, *Unspoken: A Rhetoric of Silence*. Southern Illinois University Press, 2004. p3.
11. Audre Lorde, 'The Transformation of Silence into Language and Action'. In *Sister Outsider*. Crossing Press, 2007. p41.
12. Gayatri Chakravorty Spivak, 'Can the Subaltern Speak?'. In *Can the Subaltern Speak?: Reflections on the History of an Idea*, edited by Rosalind C. Morris, Columbia University Press, 2010. p40.

13 Jeffrey McDaniel, 'The Quiet World'. In *The Forgiveness Parade*. Manic D Press, 1998. p45.
14 Ann Cvetkovich, *An Archive of Feelings: Trauma, Sexuality, and Lesbian Public Cultures*. Duke University Press, 2003. p29.
15 "Medium of Instruction: Guidance for Secondary Schools." Hong Kong Education Bureau, September 1997, edb.gov.hk/en/edu-system/primary-secondary/applicable-to-secondary/moi/guidance-index.html. Accessed 23 December 2024.
16 Ibid.
17 K. M. A. Barnett, *Hong Kong Report on the 1961 Census, Volume II*. Hong Kong Government Press, 1962. pXLVII.
18 *2021 Population Census – Summary Results*. Hong Kong Census and Statistics Department, 2022. p8.
19 Evans, S. (2011). Historical and comparative perspectives on the medium of instruction in Hong Kong. Language Policy, 10, 19-36. p21. doi.org/10.1007/s10993-011-9193-8
20 Deborah Ho, Personal interview. 17 July 2024.
21 "Recruitment of Native-speaking English Teachers (NETs) for Secondary Schools." Hong Kong Education Bureau, July 2024, edb.gov.hk/en/sch-admin/admin/about-sch-staff/net-scheme/recruitment-secondary-net.html. Accessed 23 December 2024.
22 Li, W. (2020). Multilingual English users' linguistic innovation. World Englishes, 1-13. p3. doi.org/10.1111/weng.12457
23 Rey Chow, *Not Like a Native Speaker: On Languaging as a Postcolonial Experience*. Columbia University Press, 2014. p58.
24 "Medium of Instruction: Guidance for Secondary Schools." Hong Kong Education Bureau, September 1997, edb.gov.hk/en/edu-system/primary-secondary/applicable-to-secondary/moi/guidance-index.html. Accessed 23 December 2024.
25 Edward Said, *Reflections on Exile and Other Essays*. Granta Books, 2013. p512.
26 Ngũgĩ wa Thiong'o, *Decolonising the Mind: The Politics of Language in African Literature*. James Currey, 1987. p11.
27 Lin, A. (2013). Towards Paradigmatic Change in TESOL

	Methodologies: Building Plurilingual Pedagogies from the Ground Up. TESOL Quarterly, 47:3, 521-545. p540. doi.org/10.1002/tesq.113
28	Wong, Y. & Translated by Jennifer Feeley. (2024). Overseas Bride. Chinese Literature and Thought Today, 55:1-2, 51-52. p51. doi.org/10.1080/27683524.2024.2321106
29	Lin, A. (2013). Towards Paradigmatic Change in TESOL Methodologies: Building Plurilingual Pedagogies from the Ground Up. TESOL Quarterly, 47:3, 521-545. p524-525; 538. doi.org/10.1002/tesq.113
30	*Hong Kong Advanced Level Examination 2011: Use of English – Section B Writing*. Hong Kong Examinations and Assessment Authority, 2011.
31	Ngũgĩ wa Thiong'o, *Decolonising the Mind: The Politics of Language in African Literature*. James Currey, 1987. p17-18.
32	Pennycook, A. 'From Translanguaging to Translingual Activism'. In *Decolonising Foreign Language Education: The Misteaching of English and Other Colonial Languages*, edited by Donaldo Macedo, 169–85. Routledge, 2019.
33	Yural-Davis, N. (2006). Belonging and the politics of belonging. Patterns of Prejudice, 40:3, 197-214. p197. doi.org/10.1080/00313220600769331
34	Richard Kearney, 'Introduction: Ricoeur's Philosophy of Translation'. In *On Translation*, by Paul Ricoeur, translated by Eileen Brennan. Routledge, 2006. pxiv-xv.
35	Noëlle McAfee, *Julia Kristeva*. Routledge, 2004. p34-35.
36	Ibid.
37	Lawrence Venuti, *The Translator's Invisibility: A History of Translation*. Routledge, 1995. p1.
38	Angel Pang, Personal interview. 21 August 2024.
39	Ngũgĩ wa Thiong'o, *Decolonising the Mind: The Politics of Language in African Literature*. James Currey, 1987. p17-18.
40	Richard Kearney, 'Introduction: Ricoeur's Philosophy of Translation'. In *On Translation*, by Paul Ricoeur, translated by Eileen Brennan. Routledge, 2006. pxx.
41	"To Speak Is To Blunder" Yiyun Li, *The New Yorker*, 25 December 2016. newyorker.com/magazine/2017/01/02/to-speak-is-to-blunder. Accessed 10 May 2024.

42 Yasemin Yildiz, *Beyond the Mother Tongue: The Postmonolingual Condition*. Fordham University Press, 2012. p204-205.
43 Ibid.
44 Randall, S. (1997). The Translator's Task, Walter Benjamin (Translation). TTR: Traduction, Terminologie, Rédaction, 10.2, 151-165. p161. doi.org/10.7202/037302ar
45 Paul Ricoeur. *On Translation*. Translated by Eileen Brennan. Routledge, 2006. p10.
46 Ibid. p6.
47 Cogo, A, & Fang, F. & Kordia, S. & Sifakis, N. & Siqueira, D. S. (2021). Developing ELF research for critical language education, AILA Review, 34, 187-211. p189. doi.org/10.1075/aila.21007.cog
48 Mikhail Bakhtin. 'Discourse in the Novel'. In *The Dialogic Imagination: Four Essays*. University of Texas Press, 1981. p262-263.
49 Mary Oliver, 'Praying'. In *Thirst*. Beacon Press, 2007.
50 Audre Lorde, 'The Transformation of Silence into Language and Action'. In *Sister Outsider*. Crossing Press, 2007. p40-41.
51 Ibid. p42.
52 Cym Henry, Personal interview. 5 August 2024.
53 Rose Tsui, Personal interview. 2 August 2024.
54 Paul Ricoeur, *On Translation*. Translated by Eileen Brennan. Routledge, 2006. p32.
55 Al-Saji, A. 'A Phenomenology of Hesitation: Interrupting Racializing Habits of Seeing'. In *Living Alterities: Phenomenology, Embodiment, and Race*, edited by Emily S. Lee, 133–72. p136, 140. State University of New York Press, 2014.
56 Gemma Corradi Fiurama, *The Other Side of Language: A Philosophy of Listening*. Routledge, 1990. p108.
57 James Baldwin, 'Why I Stopped Hating Shakespeare'. In *The Cross of Redemption: Uncollected Writings*. Vintage Books, 2010.

Acknowledgements

It still feels like a dream that I have written a book, and I am deeply grateful to all the people who supported and believed in me throughout this journey.

Thank you to Laura Jones-Rivera, Heather McDaid, and the 404 Ink team for believing in the idea of this book and bringing it to life; and to Luke Bird for visualising silence so beautifully.

Thank you to my interviewees – Angel Pang, Deborah Ho, Cym Henry of the Migration Museum, and Rose Tsui of the Discover Children's Story Centre – for sharing your stories and views with me, which broadened the book's perspective.

Thank you to Karen Cheung, Melitta von Pflug, and Gwendoline Choi for cherishing my words and offering invaluable feedback on the fragments and drafts that became this book. I am also grateful to all the fellow writers and researchers from my Chinese and English writing communities, as well as my friends from the On Purpose network, who expanded my world and encouraged my writing and thinking.

Thank you to Julianne, Sze Pui, Mehmeh, Ronli, Angel, Alyse, Lara, Andrea, Seetha, Michelle, Chelsea, Crystal, Ed, Monica, and to Oi Yin, Ka Lun, and Ho Ting Hei again (you know it's different when I call you by these names). It is your kindness and wisdom that empower me to keep writing.

My ballb and MoTH families: thank you for being the inspirational people that you are, and for shaping me into who I am.

Thank you to my mum, for teaching me that softness is a strength; and to my dad, for giving me the courage to know myself. You are the reason I wrote this book.

Finally, SY, thank you for simply being you. With you, everything feels possible, and everywhere feels like home.

About the Author

Wing Lam Tong (湯穎琳) is a writer, comparatist, and lawyer from Hong Kong, currently living in London. Writing in both Chinese and English, her work has appeared in *Voice & Verse Poetry Magazine*, the Asia Art Archive's *IDEAS Journal*, *The Oxonian Review*, and elsewhere. She holds a BA (Literary Studies) and LLB from the University of Hong Kong, and a Master's in Women's, Gender, and Sexuality Studies from the University of Oxford. Her research and writing explore womanhood, in-betweenness, senses of belonging, and everyday life. She believes in finding strength in softness.

About the Inklings series

This book is part of 404 Ink's Inkling series which presents big ideas in pocket-sized books.

They are all available at 404ink.com/shop.

If you enjoyed this book, you may also enjoy these titles in the series:

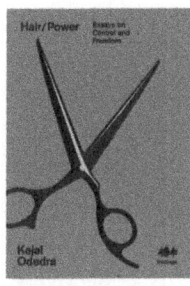

Hair/Power – Kajal Odedra

Hair is potent. Its presence and its absence has profound influence upon our lives, across race, gender, sexuality, status, and more. Odedra considers how hair has shaped society today, from the 'perfect' blondes in the school playground to the angry skinheads on the streets. Mohawks, wigs, afros, these are just a few of the ways in which hair has been part of history and wider activism.

BFFs – Anahit Behrooz

Friendships can be the foundation of our earliest memories and most formative moments. But why are they often seen as secondary to romantic, or familial connection, something to age out of and take a back seat to other relationships? BFFs is an examination of the power of female friendship, not as something lesser, but as a site of radical intimacy, as told through the cultural touchstones around us.

Look, Don't Touch – layla-roxanne hill & Francesca Sobande

Look, Don't Touch journeys through the music of feeling, "self-help" social media, the power of public signage, and more to call for a move away from the language of "okayness", and a move towards collectively uplifting forms of anger, agitation, love, solidarity, release, and ultimately, *feeling*.